# THE LANGUAGE OF CONTEMPORARY CRITICISM CLARIFIED

William Innes Homer

UNIVERSITY OF DELAWARE

To Jacqui and Fred
with love
Bill

SOUND VIEW PRESS

1999

*To my brother and sister-in-law*
*Steve and Florence Homer*


By the Same Author:

*Seurat and the Science of Painting*
(MIT Press)

*Robert Henri and His Circle*
(Cornell University Press)

*Alfred Stieglitz and the American Avant-Garde*
(New York Graphic Society)

*Alfred Stieglitz and the Photo-Secession*
(New York Graphic Society)

*Albert Pinkham Ryder: Painter of Dreams* (with Lloyd Goodrich)
(Harry N. Abrams, Inc.)

*Thomas Eakins: His Life and Art*
(Abbeville Press)

© 1999 by William Innes Homer

Published in the United States of America by
Sound View Press
P. O. Box 833
Madison, CT 06443
Telephone: 203-245-2246 • Fax: 203-245-5116
email: info@falkart.com
Internet bookstore: www.falkart.com


ISBN 0-932087-58-2

# Contents

INTRODUCTION                                                7

ACKNOWLEDGMENTS                                            10

CHAPTER 1.   MARXIST CRITICISM
             Karl Marx                                     12
             Marxism and Marxism-Leninism                  14
             Marx and Engels: Aesthetic Views             16
             Western Marxism
                  Georg Lukács                             18
                  Antonio Gramsci                          19
             The Frankfurt School                          21
                  Walter Benjamin                          24
                  Theodor Adorno                           26

CHAPTER 2.   STRUCTURALISM AND ITS AFTERMATH
             Saussure and Semiotic Structuralism           29
             Russian Formalism and the Prague School       33
             Claude Lévi-Strauss                           35

CHAPTER 3.   FROM STRUCTURALISM TO DECONSTRUCTION
             AND BEYOND
             Michel Foucault                               38
             Roland Barthes                                42
             Jacques Derrida                               49
             Jacques Lacan                                 55
             Jean-François Lyotard                         59
             Jean Baudrillard                              65

CHAPTER 4.   POSTSTRUCTURALISM AND POSTMODERNISM
             Poststructuralism                             69
             Postmodernism                                 73

*CONTINUED*

**CHAPTER 5.** **ALTERNATIVE VIEWS**

Mikhail Bakhtin 80

Jürgen Habermas 83

Louis Althusser 85

**CHAPTER 6.** **CURRENT APPROACHES**

Cultural Studies 88

Feminism 92

Visual Culture 95

**CHAPTER 7.** **CONCLUSION** 99

**CHAPTER 8.** **GLOSSARY** 101

# INTRODUCTION

The worlds of art, culture, history, and criticism have been invaded, in recent times, by arcane language and a set of confusing theoretical concepts. Texts that follow this kind of approach — and there are many — are difficult to read and comprehend. Indeed they often can be understood only by the knowledgeable minority that knows the code. Yet it is essential for thinking people on the outside, especially students, to find the key to this unfamiliar world. I have written this book to provide such a key.

This volume consists of two sections that are closely related to each other. The first is a series of text essays written by me that explain larger concepts such as structuralism and poststructuralism, movements like the Frankfurt School, or the teachings of influential thinkers from Marx to Althusser. These essays are meant to explain the complexities of modern and postmodern theoretical and critical writing. But they also serve as background and context for the second section of the book, an extensive glossary of currently relevant terminology.

When I first confronted the more difficult terms that appear in the glossary — words like ludic, reflexivity, bricolage, heuristic, reify, homology, and indexicality — I consulted my dictionary. But even when I looked them up, I was not satisfied. The definitions were either imperfect, out of date, or nonexistent. Frustrated, I turned to specialized reference works that dealt with technical terms in literary criticism, linguistics, social theory, and philosophy. Yet they often did not provide definitions that conformed to current (or currently fashionable) usage.

Moreover, when theorists use these words, they often take on a new, expanded meaning. Like elements in chemistry, they possess a "valence," or capacity to combine or react with one another. This trait may be strongly positive or strongly negative, or somewhere in between. In other words, the concepts signified by these terms reflect a culture or pattern of thought prized by current theorists — or disparaged by them. This language, then, is not absolute, but carries definite political-theoretical connotations. My task (shared with my collaborators acknowledged in the glossary) has been not only to define these terms but also to ferret out their unwritten meanings.

The starting point for this book is the theoretical thinking of Karl Marx. The kind of criticism he inspired actually flourished about the same time that formalism came into prominence in the early twentieth century, but it took a while longer for Marx's theory to gain a foothold. Like formalism, it continues as a dominant current, even to the present day.

The next major units of critical thinking — structuralism, deconstruction, and poststructuralism — are different from Marxist and formalist criticism, though at times they intersect with them. Deconstruction and poststructuralism also merge with and become part of the concept of postmodernism, which will be dealt with separately, in contrast to modernism.

Finally, I will cover the main tenets of Cultural Studies, an approach that has become quite popular within the past few years, as well as feminism, and visual culture, all very much at the forefront of thinking today.

In the text of this book, I have tried to make complex ideas easy to understand. I have used language that is, as much as possible, nontechnical and liberated from jargon. The reader will discover that deconstructive and poststructural theorists seem to fear logic and often engage in purposeful obfuscation. I do not believe, however, that one must adopt the same verbal strategies when discussing the ideas of these thinkers, or any others. Admittedly, in some cases, my explanatory language may fail to do justice to these authors' sense of nuance and poetic ambiguity. But I believe logical, sequential thought is necessary if one is to break through the barriers of obscurity.

Many disciplines — art criticism, linguistics, literary theory, anthropology, social theory, philosophy, and psychoanalysis — are represented in this book. Overlapping and merging, sometimes one will be linked to another and at a different time two, three, four, or more will be brought into play. The result is often an amalgam — for example, linguistics, literary criticism, and philosophy — that has no fixed disciplinary focus. But indeed a variety of disciplines have come to influence critics and historians, along with artists, over the past several decades and therefore must be wrestled with.

After reading countless volumes of theory and having found how difficult they are to understand, I wonder if there is not, somewhere, an unwritten policy of encapsulating theoretical ideas in an arcane coded language. Facing this situation, I have not only tried to break the code but also to open this world to others, especially those who are looking at or thinking about creative production — visual or verbal, historical or contemporary. Thus, it is my hope that readers will be helped in their encounters with the confusing conceptual language and terminology that flourish in our time.

# ACKNOWLEDGMENTS

In the course of preparing to teach a seminar on postmodernism in 1991, I delved into a challenging body of theoretical writing that I wanted my students to read. When I reviewed this material, I concluded that much of the language and terminology would be unfamiliar and hard for them to understand. Therefore, as a group project, I assigned each student one or more terms and asked him or her to define each of them broadly and clearly in a few paragraphs. When these definitions were completed, I assembled them as a glossary for the readings we were to do in the course. The fruits of this exercise proved to be so valuable that I thought the results ought to be published. I believed there must be others all over the country — indeed, around the world — who would benefit from this guide to obscure and troubling terminology. So, with many additional entries by myself, graduate students Tracy Myers and Allan Antliff, and seminar students in a similar course in the fall of 1995, the glossary at the end of this book took its present form.

The name of the student author, or my own when appropriate, is cited at the end of each entry. Each student has given permission for his or her essay to be published in this collective project.

I would also like to acknowledge the advice of the following individuals with whom I discussed the content of the book: Mark Amsler, Aline Brandauer, Linn Dietrich, Patricia Leighten, and Elaine Safer. Margaret Hassert skillfully edited the manuscript; I am particularly grateful for the thoughtful care she gave to this task. During the course of this project, I employed several research assistants whose talent and hard work I wish to recognize: Allan Antliff, Heather Campbell, Beth Hinderliter, and Rebecca Weller.

My agent, Regina Ryan, was very helpful in giving shape to the project and made a number of useful editorial suggestions.

Finally, I wish to acknowledge the very real help of my wife Christine, who discussed the ideas of the book with me, read the manuscript, and provided encouragement and support at every turn.

WILLIAM INNES HOMER
July 1, 1999

# CHAPTER 1
# MARXIST CRITICISM

## Karl Marx

The views of Karl Marx (1818-1888) on political reform, social theory, and revolution have exerted vast influence throughout the world. But when we think of Marx, the fine arts do not leap to mind. Yet his ideas were so abundant and compelling that they easily spilled over into the realm of art and literary criticism and thus inspired successive generations of Marxian intellectuals. Although we will not be concerned with his socioeconomic theories for their own sake, the general development of these ideas and those of his followers need to be cited as background for Marxist aesthetics and criticism.

The Industrial Revolution, a direct product of the capitalist system, created the oppressive social conditions that Marx felt obliged to attack. These evils centered on the exploitation of the workers (members of the proletarian class) by the owners of the means of production (capitalists), who belonged to the bourgeois class. The factory, where laborers found themselves alienated and detached from their own products, was the center of the conflict between these classes.

Because the dominant non-laboring capitalists held the power, the only way for the working-class producers to escape from oppression was to rebel, to overthrow capitalism and the bourgeois society that supported it. Revolutionary action by the proletariat was thus seen as inevitable. The ultimate goal was a classless and stateless society that was to be reached after going through a transitional period called the dictatorship of the proletariat (or proletarian democracy). Only by taking these steps, Marx thought, could the exploitation of the proletariat be halted. The end result would be a harmonious, humane society. Rational planning and cooperation would help achieve his goals. Religion, however, would have no place in the system.

Marx formulated a convincing theoretical apparatus, especially in his monumental work *Capital* (1867, 1889, 1894), that would support his social goals and persuade others of their worth. Underlying all of his thinking was the economic motive. Every social system is built upon a mode of production (that is, its economic "base," or way of producing things), and that base in turn is directly responsible for the emergence of a set of secondary beliefs in society (the "superstructure") — political, aesthetic, legal, and intellectual. To change the superstructure in any society, Marx believed, the primary economic base would have to be altered.

Marx viewed society as an organic whole, analogous to "nature" and subject to practical scientific laws like those of physics, chemistry, and biology. Even history had a kind of scientific inevitability or sense of "progress" about it. History, like everything else Marx considered, unfolded in a dialectical process, following the philosopher Georg Wilhelm Friedrich Hegel, but without his metaphysics (hence Marx's term "dialectical materialism"). The present, Marx thought, grew organically out of the past and was largely determined by it. But the future triumph of a classless society was also governed by this dialectic because it was the continuation of a progressive series of conflicts or revolutions that led to the collapse of bourgeois capitalism. The principles of "historical materialism," a term favored by Marx and his collaborator Friedrich Engels, undergirded this development, following a kind of history that is fashioned by man as a social being, not by any divine or supernatural forces.

## Marxism and Marxism-Leninism

The socioeconomic principles and view of history set forth by Marx changed in the hands of his immediate and more distant followers. As is true of any seminal thinker, his theories were so rich and multi-faceted that his successors could easily develop different or even opposing ideas. In the following paragraphs, we will briefly outline how, when, and where others articulated and altered Marx's thoughts as a background for the emergence of Marxist criticism.

Friedrich Engels (1820-1895) was one of the leaders of Marxism after the death of Marx. Engels saw to it that the second and third volumes of Marx's *Capital* were published (1889, 1894) and helped give shape to the Second International (1889-1914), a loose confederation of Marxist parties and trade unions in which the German Social Democrats played a leading role. Through the International, socialism was promoted on a massive scale. After Engels' death in 1895, many debates ensued, and these set a pattern for the continuing arguments within Marxism that have persisted to the present day.

A major landmark in the history of Marxism was Russia's large-scale adoption of a Marxian ideology. This happened largely through the efforts of Lenin (1870-1924), a convinced Russian Marxist who advanced the cause of socialist revolution. By October 1917, thanks largely to him, the Marxist principle of unifying the workers to seize power forcefully bore fruit: The Russian Revolution, dominated by Lenin's Bolsheviks, became a success. This event, Lenin hoped, would be a model for the socialist revolutions around the world.

It was but a short step — though there was some opposition — from revolution to the creation of a Marxist-Leninist state in Russia. Lenin had provided the necessary Marxist ideology and erected a practical framework that strengthened the hand of his party, silencing the opposition as he went along. And when Joseph Stalin, after Lenin's

14

death in 1924, gained absolute control in 1929, the Soviet Union was able to transform Leninism into a massive exercise in authoritarian power. Stalin believed, in contrast to his rival, Leon Trotsky, that the Soviet Union should constitute itself as the model socialist state and that world revolution could wait.

The Soviet state under Stalin's domineering leadership became a frozen caricature of Marx's humane goals and a gross exaggeration of Lenin's belief in centralized party power. In his compulsive effort to prove that the Soviet Union could outstrip the capitalist system, Stalin made the nation adopt a system of collective farming and forced his countrymen to industrialize. The state took precedence over everything else, and to preserve its power Stalin indulged in cruel repression, coercion, and mass murder — whatever it took to accomplish his goals. His public aims came to be identified more and more with his personal autocratic rule.

When one thinks of art and aesthetics in the Soviet Union, "socialist realism" immediately comes to mind. That style was prescribed under Stalin's regime, and anything else was discouraged. Socialist realism was meant to reflect faithfully (hence the term "reflectionism") the state of the working classes and of society in the Soviet Union. Art of this kind was designed to be understood by all; thus, veracity of style was expected to parallel a realistic subject matter. Commonly encountered was propaganda for the noble accomplishments of the State. Art thus became academic, a "correct" and fossilized echo of socially responsive and responsible expression of the kind that Marx himself, for example, enjoyed.

## Marx and Engels:  Aesthetic Views

Karl Marx never published a coherent theory of art or aesthetics, nor did his collaborator Engels.  But the two revolutionaries did enjoy certain kinds of art and literature.  Both, for instance, admired Raphael, with Leonardo and Titian being close runners-up, because all three were commendable products of their social milieus — Rome, Florence, and Venice, respectively.  Raphael, however, was not enough of a realist, Marx and Engels felt; preferably, artists should capture the reality of their subjects in affirmative, Rembrandt-like tones.  In literature, the pair cherished Balzac for his realism, Carlyle for his anti-bourgeois stance, and Heinrich Heine for his sympathetic view of utopian socialism.

Marx, who possessed a greater knowledge of the fine arts than Engels, thought Greek art was the supreme achievement.  He praised it especially because it reflected a democratic (his early word for communist) society.  In literature, he favored the poetry of Aeschylus and Shakespeare, along with the writings of Dante, Cervantes, and Lessing as much for personal enjoyment as for any social message they may have conveyed.  He did find such a social content, however, in his reading of the realistic novels of Dickens, Thackeray, Charlotte Brontë, and Mrs. Gaskell.

Engels, though not unfamiliar with art, had a strong preference for music.  He thought Beethoven was a superb composer, an opinion that might seem startling, at first, given his (Engels') revolutionary socialism.  But, as Donald Drew Egbert has pointed out, music, especially as performed by full orchestras, "to socialists and communists could connote collective harmony" (Egbert, 79).  Music, like art, was also shaped by its milieu; the individual composer would thus be swept along by the conditions of his own time and place.  Engels, in association with Marx, observed that, to quote Egbert, "Mozart's *Requiem* could be successfully completed by another composer under the same social conditions" (ibid.).

All in all, however, Marx and Engels did not place a very high value on art in their revolutionary designs for a new society. Art of the present day would be part of the superstructure but did not enjoy a elevated rank therein. The individual artist was merged into a larger societal picture, where he could serve the goals of socialist revolution. Art was not to become a commodity, a medium of exchange, or a luxury to be savored for its own sake.

# Western Marxism

## Georg Lukács

Georg (Gyorgy) Lukács (1885-1971) has been called the first major Marxist philosopher of the twentieth century. In addition, he was a talented literary critic and persuasive social theorist. An independent intellectual from bourgeois roots, Lukács in the earlier part of his career offered a humane, flexible interpretation of Marxist doctrine. At the start, it was the early, "humanistic" Marx that interested him, the Marx who had absorbed and drawn upon the philosophy of Hegel. From Hegel, in turn, Lukács adopted an approach that stressed the idea of organic totality, a situation in which all facets of the human endeavor interacted, the sum being more important than the parts. This view offered an antidote to the fragmentation of life in which man felt alienated. Also Hegelian was Lukács' belief that a larger historical and political context governs the individual's artistic and intellectual creations; economics was no longer the principal determining factor in human affairs.

Lukács thought the arts should be grounded in the social, political, and physical reality of the material world. But he did not follow the orthodox Marxist theory of reflectionism, for he believed the individual creator could transform the real world in the course of interpreting it. For example, he admired the writings of Sir Walter Scott, Charles Dickens, Stendhal, Honoré de Balzac, and Leo Tolstoy — even though they spoke for a bourgeois culture — because they realistically and skillfully represented people in actual social situations, whether past or present. The proletarian writer, he thought, could learn something from them, rather than succumb to the stereotyped propaganda of socialist realism. Like the orthodox (Soviet) Marxists, but for different reasons, he did not tolerate modernist experimentation in the arts. Modernists were out of touch with the proletariat, who, he thought, would find modern creative production "subjective, confused, and disfigured" (quoted in Lunn, 82). Thus, Lukács promoted realistic art that was relevant and close to the people, not confusing to them.

Lukács' viewpoint was far too individualistic and flexible — even humanistic — for the arbiters of Soviet aesthetics. His Hegelian phase, in particular, was condemned by orthodox Marxist-Leninists as being romantic and bourgeois, and he was pressured to abandon his earlier positions outlined in his influential book, *History and Class Consciousness* (1923). By the 1920s and '30s, he was ensconced in the conservative Soviet camp and recanted much of what he had written before. Yet *History and Class Consciousness* exerted considerable influence on later Western Marxists, and his writings and example laid a foundation for the Frankfurt School. That group of thinkers echoed and developed his critical, questioning approach to the arts and society, and some shared his belief that a dominant ideology permeates all levels of human endeavor.

### Antonio Gramsci

Antonio Gramsci (1891-1937) has been called "the first self-conscious 'Western Marxist' " (Jay, 1984, 163). A philosopher and political theorist, he was also engaged in politics, first as a socialist activist, then, in 1924, as an organizer of the Italian Communist Party. He became head of the Party in 1924 but was jailed in 1926 when Benito Mussolini's fascists gained control of the country and outlawed communists. Although Gramsci spent eleven years in prison — he died in 1937, just after his release — he was able to write voluminously on philosophy, political theory, culture (including art, literature, theater), and especially the concept of hegemony, the theme for which he is best known. These writings were published posthumously as the *Prison*

*Notebooks* in 1948-51, with English editions coming out in 1975. Because of the delay in getting this material into print, Gramsci was little recognized until after World War II. Today, he is hailed as a key figure in cultural and social theory.

Gramsci's ideas on hegemony are linked to his concept of society. Steering away from orthodox (materialist) Marxism, he embraced, under the influence of the Italian philosopher Benedetto Croce, a humanist view of Marx's teachings. Gramsci also appreciated the Hegelian-Marxist idea of totality that pictures society as an organic entity. But he did not pay attention, as Marx had done, to economic motives. To influence and change society, Gramsci believed one would have to work with a broad spectrum of ideas — cultural, political, and moral. It is here, in these mutually reinforcing domains, that hegemonic power resides, a power that can shape and direct society. Hegemony, Gramsci discovered, had served capitalism as a tool to control the masses. That equation, though, was reversible: the proletariat could be educated in the benefits of socialism and transformed by these same means. Intellectuals and artists, linking themselves to the masses, would play a significant role in this task. Even folklore and popular culture could exert a beneficial social influence.

Influenced by Hegelian Marxism (and paralleling Lukács), Gramsci saw history as an organic totality that incorporated all facets of social activity. As he said, "Poetics and economics, environment and social organisms are always one" (quoted in Jay, 1984, 153). History, moreover, unfolds in progressive steps, moving ever forward toward increasing freedom. Although, according to Gramsci, history has a rhythm and energy of its own, individuals can also change the course of events, a view that was unpopular with orthodox Marxists, who submerged the individual within the social system.

Even though few scholars have commented on Gramsci's aesthetic, literary, and critical views, he did write on these matters, albeit in a fragmentary and inconsistent way. Like Lukács (though probably without being influenced by him), he wanted to formulate a Marxian aesthetic credo, one that sidestepped the strict economic, scientific Marx in favor of a thoughtful critical appraisal of the arts in society. Literature, in particular, would exert a beneficial influence on people's ideologies and, indeed, on the entire progress of history as an organic entity. Intellectuals and artists would play a crucial role in this effort. Gramsci, however, parted company with Lukács in supporting the kind of modernism that Lukács condemned. Too, Gramsci turned his back on high art from time to time and like Walter Benjamin (probably without knowing that theorist's work) examined the effects of popular taste and mass culture on the populace.

Gramsci's eleven years in prison isolated him, though not entirely, from the development of Western Marxist political thinking. Yet it is surprising, as Renate Holub points out, how closely he parallels Lukács and the Frankfurt School. His treatment of semiotics and linguistics, she observes, also anticipates post-World-War-II structuralism, and his allusive counter-hegemonic language even foreshadows poststructuralism (ibid., 20-21). His critical assessment of the artist in relation to society and history, on the other hand, relates to the discipline of Cultural Studies. Thus, it is not surprising to see a vigorous revival of interest today in this once obscure thinker.


## The Frankfurt School

The Frankfurt School consisted of a group of influential social theorists and critics, some of whom were also philosophers, who gathered under the banner of the Institut für Sozialforschung (Institute for Social Research) in Frankfurt, Germany. Founded in 1923 at the University of Frankfurt, this research institute played host to, among others, Max

Horkheimer (who became director in 1931), Theodor W. Adorno, Walter Benjamin, Herbert Marcuse (well known later in the United States for his book *One Dimensional Man*), and Erich Fromm. Almost all Jewish, these and other members were indebted in different ways to Marx's teachings, but as neo-Marxists they developed a research program called "critical theory" that kept them clear of direct political action. This phrase, popularized by Horkheimer, is not easy to define. Nonetheless, we can tease a core meaning out of it. "Critical" refers broadly to the use of "critique" as a way of dealing with problems. Critique is a philo-sophical sort of inquiry appropriated by Marx and his followers to ana-lyze the necessary conditions for various kinds of concepts and prac-tices, especially in the political-social domain. As to "theory," this is an echo of the Marxian demand for a rational, theoretical underpinning for a set of systematic truths that will form a blueprint for practice (or praxis). In the case of the Frankfurt School, as with the Western Marxists, revolutionary action took second place to theoretical specula-tion. As Marcuse said: "Theory will preserve the truth even if revolu-tionary practice deviates from its proper path. Practice follows the truth, not vice versa" (*Reason and Revolution,* quoted in Jay, 1973, 79). (To further complicate matters the words "critical theory" came to be used, from the late 1960s to the present in a very different manner. In that case, it referred essentially to the intellectual activity of the decon-structionists and poststructuralists, mostly French, whom we will discuss later.)

Although the members of the Frankfurt School were generally hos-tile to capitalism, they also disliked Soviet Communism under Stalin as well as Hitler's Germany. Both of these national systems were totalitari-an, and thus earned the scorn of the Frankfurt School. Too, the Frankfurt theorists moved away from the later Marx's materialistic or science-based philosophy to take up issues of literature, art, aesthetics, psychology, and popular culture in relation to society. These topics were particularly appealing, in an escapist way, to those pessimistic members who believed that the social order was beyond redemption. But other adherents felt the Frankfurt School should be an inspiring beacon for the freedom of the individual in the face of dark, authoritarian forces.

The Frankfurt Institute for Social Research opposed Hitler's fascism. Hitler, in turn, had no time for the left-wing Frankfurt group, closed down the Institute in 1933, and drove the members into exile. A group of Institute colleagues established themselves in Geneva, Switzerland, then in New York City, at Columbia University, in 1936. After the war, in 1950, several of the key members, including Horkheimer and Adorno, returned to Frankfurt, where the Institute reopened and continued to sponsor further research on critical theory until 1973, when it closed down.

A star of this second generation was the neo-Marxist Jürgen Habermas, Adorno's assistant and a talented philosopher and social theorist in his own right, who developed and expanded the Frankfurt School tradition in the 1960s and following decades, right up to the present. The value of his work will be discussed later on.

Although the Institute members were called a "school," it would be a mistake to see them as the designers of a monolithic belief system. Rather, they were linked by a few broad assumptions which each interpreted in his own way. They would agree, for instance, that their approach, in the spirit of the liberal side of Marx, would have to be "critical" or probing — not doctrinaire or closed. By the same token, they used reason to shape a philosophical theory, or theories, that would help them wrestle with the social and cultural issues of their time. The Frankfurt School represented a revolution of the intellect, its adherents believing in change, liberated thought, and emancipation. Members, however, did not always agree with each other. Adorno and Benjamin, for example, frequently engaged in vigorous debates.

During the years of its existence in Frankfurt, the group was not particularly well known. Their influence, however, became widespread in the 1960s and continues to grow. The names of Adorno and Benjamin, in particular, appear again and again in current theoretical texts. And while the Marxist leanings of the Frankfurt intellectuals might seem foreign to the poststructuralists, there is growing evidence that the former group exerted direct and indirect influence on the latter. Of course, the Frankfurt School's ties with Marxist ideas made them appealing to latter-day Marxist historians and critics of the New Left.

### Walter Benjamin

A neo-Marxist literary critic and philosopher associated with the Frankfurt school, Walter Benjamin (1892-1940) was little known when he produced his major writings in the 1920s and '30s. He became a culture hero only after he was "discovered" in the 1960s. His thinking influenced New Left activists in that decade and the next, and he foreshadowed and affected some of the deconstructionist critics of the 1970s and 1980s. Hannah Arendt has called him "the most important German literary critic between the two wars" (Egbert, 682).

In his early years as a scholar, Benjamin directed his critical eye especially to Baroque and modern literature. He believed that the arts should be evaluated as a product of their historical milieu, but he avoided systems of classifying and arranging historical data. Instead, he worked with small details, fragments that he assembled loosely in "constellations." This method allowed him to respect and respond to the work of art without its becoming lost in a rigid, conceptual system.

Benjamin moved from these interests toward Marxism in the late 1920s, drawing inspiration directly from the writings of Marx and Lukács. Benjamin went to Moscow in the winter of 1926-27 and contemplated joining the Communist Party, but did not. Having no affiliation with a university, he earned a meager living as a journalist, principally writing critical appraisals of literature. But he was fortunate in being able to affiliate himself with the Frankfurt Institute for Social Research and thus developed friendships with, among others, Theodor Adorno. Benjamin also came to know the playwright Bertolt Brecht, whose notions of the social grounding of the work of art influenced Benjamin.

While Benjamin adopted some of the tenets of Marxism, principally that art mirrors the condition of society and that aesthetics and politics are intimately related, he was also an independent critical thinker. Rather than accept the neo-Hegelian idea of social and historical totality, Benjamin stood apart from anything that threatened to become a system. Indeed, two related sources that influenced him — Surrealism and Freud — by nature lack a controlling theoretical foundation. Thus, it is not surprising that they appealed to Benjamin.

In 1936, Benjamin set forth his ideas on popular culture in his best known and frequently cited essay, "The Work of Art in an Age of Mechanical Reproduction." He praised the idea that original works of art made prior to his own time radiate an authentic "aura," an idea, Martin Jay points out, that was frequently heard at the Frankfurt Institute (Jay, 1973, 210). The unique art object, too, embodies the historic or traditional roots from which it stems. But as we enter the age in which mechanical reproduction flourishes, there is a cultural crisis, and the aura is lost. As Benjamin said: "The instant the criterion of authenticity ceases to be applicable to artistic production, the total function of art is reversed. Instead of being based on ritual, it begins to be based on another practice — politics" (quoted in Jay, 1973, 210). Mechanically reproduced cultural products, including film, had the power to control the thinking of the masses and thus could bolster movements like fascism, keeping people satisfied with their present condition. The orthodox Frankfurt School view, exemplified by Adorno, feared this situation. But Benjamin saw some good in it, saying that mass-produced art, a Chaplin film for example, might collectively lead people toward more understanding than a painting by Picasso. Such thoughts of Benjamin — openly accepting popular culture — were ahead of their time because they foreshadowed the rise of Pop Art and the recent attention given to the popular arts by adherents of the academic discipline known as Cultural Studies (to be discussed later).

As we look back at Benjamin, he seems to be a bifurcated personality. He was at once a materialist Marxist, whose writings were in various ways politicized, and also something of a Jewish mystic, a cabalist, to borrow Eugene Lunn's appellation (Lunn, 179). He preferred allegory, with its fluid meanings, to fixed symbolism. And he sidestepped utilitarian language, choosing instead poetic, suggestive words that did not allow themselves to be used as instruments of logic or domination. In this and in other ways he foreshadows the deconstructionists.


## Theodor Adorno

A Frankfurt School intellectual with unusually diverse interests, Theodor Adorno (1903-1969) wrote in the fields of music and literary criticism, aesthetics, social theory, philosophy, psychology, popular culture, and the mass media. His first and most dominant love, however, was music: as a young man, he had studied musicology and composition. Not surprisingly, the structure and aesthetics of music served as the basis for his critical thinking. This may explain his willingness to look at the structural, formal aspects of the work of art as well as its place in society.

It may be easiest to define Adorno by stating, first, what he was not. He did not believe in phenomenology or existentialism, nor did he care for bourgeois humanism or any kind of metaphysics. Understandably, he despised the Nazi totalitarian regime that led to the horrors of Jewish extermination in the concentration camps. That catastrophe scarred his soul: he felt that "to write poetry after Auschwitz is barbaric" (quoted in Jay, 1984, 243). Enlightenment and reason, in principle, should have offered some hope; yet Adorno was afraid to encourage the facet of the Enlightenment that led to instrumentalism — the practical use of reason to dominate society and nature.

Adorno demonstrated an oddly divided view of "totality," a central issue among neo-Marxists. The vision of society as a whole or organic totality had been proclaimed by Lukács, and this stance, which reflected Hegel's influence, flourished among Western Marxists in Germany in the 1920s. Adorno was suspicious of this position, for he thought, influenced by his colleague Benjamin, that holistic thinking and absolute truth were philosophically undesirable. Adorno even gave up the Marxian (and Hegelian) dialectical method, asserting that opposites need not be resolved in some orderly, predictable way. Allowing tension to remain between opposing concepts, he welcomed the idea of "non-identity."

In his departure from rigorous logic, Adorno is not unlike Jacques Derrida, who promoted a similar idea of *différance* [deferral] central to deconstructive views. Lack of resolution was also linked, in Adorno's thinking, with a kind of pessimistic inaction, a feeling of impotence in the face of encroaching capitalism, on one hand, and the victories of totalitarian regimes (Nazi Germany and Soviet Russia), on the other. Even his language became fragmentary, no longer bound by a coherent system, more like "illuminations."

Although Adorno might not have admitted it, the arts, especially music, offered him an avenue of personal escape. This was not, of course, music for music's sake, because as a good neo-Marxist, Adorno felt compelled to tie that medium to social processes. But he did so not in any simplistic, descriptive, or narrative way. Rather, he drew structural analogies between the form of music and social structure. For example, in its regular and formal design, music could express "domination."

On the other hand, the compositions of avant-gardist Arnold Schönberg, so admired by Adorno, reflected a totalizing society by rejecting it, in this case through a controversial dissonant musical vocabulary.

Although Adorno believed that the arts could be linked to social goals and causes, he sidestepped the idea of art as propaganda. He attacked Lukács for his narrow-minded view of literature as a mirror of reality and by contrast opted for an open, experimental modernism, praising not only Schönberg but also writers like Baudelaire, Valéry, Proust, and Kafka. A parallel between this point of view and his faith in philosophical openness and lack of closure can easily be drawn: modernism symbolizes the resistance to conformity, a negation of logic. Needless to say, his position put him at odds with other Marxists, but in his freedom from restraint, he remains a typical member of the Frankfurt School.

Besides addressing high art, Adorno turned to still another but very different facet of culture: the popular arts, including film and radio, pulp fiction, and especially music. Unlike his colleague Benjamin, who had found some revolutionary value in these things, Adorno promoted a strict division between high and low art. The latter ought to be condemned, he felt, because it repressed and dominated the masses. As a result, people would not think or feel for themselves. America was the principal source of this kind of oppressive control, and Adorno ultimately felt defeated by the overwhelming power of the media.

# CHAPTER 2

# STRUCTURALISM AND ITS AFTERMATH

## Saussure and Semiotic Structuralism

Structuralism is a method, a point of view, and a philosophy of sorts; yet it is not limited to any single discipline. Structuralism started in linguistics, came to serve as the basis for semiotics (the science of signs), became a foundation for structural anthropology, and eventually undergirded a whole school of literary criticism. That is not all. As structuralism matured in France in the 1950s and 1960s, its influence spread from literature (both criticism and writing) to psychology, mathematics, history, philosophy, and physics. By the mid 1970s, structuralism had won out over the dominant intellectual currents of Marxism, existentialism, and phenomenology. The reasons for this victory will be dealt with later on; it is enough to say at this point that the postwar world was a fertile field for structuralism, and the movement caught on with exceptional vigor. Yet at the moment of its greatest triumph, structuralism came under attack by the poststructuralists and soon became outmoded.

The foundations of structuralism were laid shortly before the start of World War I. It has been said that structuralism responded to the conditions of the times, an epoch that witnessed a troubling fragmentation of knowledge. The different disciplines, it seemed, did not talk to each other. Yet within the individual fields there were parallel searches for order and structure, for example, in the work of the physicist Max Planck; the psychologist Wolfgang Köhler, a leading member of the Gestalt school; and Ludwig Wittgenstein, language philosopher and hero of the structuralists.

Structuralism sought totality and systems, not isolated facts. It looked for relationships between contemporaneous linguistic events, not linear historical connections between one event and another but rather links between activities that take place in the present. (Later, the structuralist method was applied to historical periods and occurrences by Michel Foucault.) The individual (the self) would be subordinated to, and become part of, a large coherent script, one so logical that it might even seem scientific.

The principal hero of the structuralists is Ferdinand de Saussure (1857-1913). He was a Swiss linguist who published little about his subject during his lifetime, but his students assembled his lecture notes, *Course in General Linguistics,* and issued it as a book in 1916. This fundamental work became something of a bible to later structuralists, including practitioners of structural linguistics.

Saussure did not look at language as a collection of separate words, each having a separate meaning, nor did he treat language as part of a changing historical evolution (diachronically). Instead, he concentrated on the relationship of the parts of the language, seeing language as a unitary or self-sufficient whole. And he dealt with language as spoken at a given moment (synchronically). As Fredric Jameson put it, "Saussure's originality was to have insisted on the fact that language as a total system is complete at every moment, no matter what happens to have been altered in it a moment before" (Jameson, 1972, 5-6). The phrase "total system" suggests that Saussure saw language as a self-contained entity in which each contributing verbal unit enjoys a relation to every other unit and to the whole. In other words, he had discovered a structure or system underlying human language, which had little or nothing to do with the origin and history of word usage.

Saussure gave specific names to the parts of language and linguistic relationships that are central to structuralist and also much of poststructuralist thought. For example, the general concept of language has two components: *langue* (language) and *parole* (speech or speaking). These two ideas relate to each other in the manner of a chess game. In chess, there is a governing grammar, rules and principles that determine the way the game is played, but we must also recognize that moves by individual contestants are a matter of free choice within the system. Thus, the concept of language is to the general rules of chess what individual words are to the specific moves in the game. As John Storey put it: "The task of structuralism is to make explicit the rules and conventions (the structure) which favored the production of meaning (the *parole*)" (Storey, 72).

Saussure believed that human beings have a natural ability to create verbal signs that correspond to ideas. This faculty, he thought, was part of a larger structure of language at a given time and place; and that very structure was the subject of his linguistic studies. Further, he thought signs consisted of two elements, the "signifier" (*signifiant*) and the "signified" (*signifié*). The signifier is the sound language or sound-image and the signified is the concept associated with the sound image. Terence Hawkes explained: "The structural relationship between the concept of a tree (i.e., the signified) and the sound-image made by the word 'tree' (i.e., the signifier) constitutes a linguistic sign." The word "tree," however, is only a sign for the object it describes; it has no tree-like qualities in and of itself. Any other word or even a nonsense syllable, Saussure believed, could signify "tree." Thus, language has, in Hawkes' words, "no 'reality' beyond itself; it constitutes its own reality" (Hawkes, 26).

According to Saussure, words gain their meaning in accordance with the larger linguistic context in which they are placed. Essential are linguistic relationships based on "differences" or opposition of sounds. Thus, the "d" in "dog" is what makes that word different from "cog" or "fog." Because of this change, the word's meaning has shifted. Similar relationships of opposition are found in the relationships between words in a sentence. According to Saussure, these ties occupy two different dimensions. One is the "horizontal," or syntagmatic, axis; and the other is the "vertical," or associative, axis. (Another word for this latter term — "paradigmatic" — is often heard but is wrongly attributed to Saussure [it is from Roman Jakobson].) Language, he points out, proceeds through time in a linear direction like a train with its many cars. Thus, a sentence like "The boy threw the ball" derives much of its meaning from the "horizontal" connection of the individual words to each other. But the "vertical" aspect can also be brought into play when there are substitutions for (or omissions of) words, one for another, in the very same position in the sentence. To use a related example, "The boy caught [instead of threw] the ball." Both aspects, the horizontal (syntagmatic) and vertical (associative), are necessary to the meaning of the sentence, and both rely on the relative position or relation of words in a linguistic system or structural network.

Saussure concerned himself with internal verbal relationships that belonged to a larger conceptual whole. He was not interested in the phenomenal world, in persons and things in nature to which words referred, nor did he involve himself with the expression of broad human values or "content." His scientific leanings prompted him to envision a new science called "semiology" (now usually called semiotics) to be devoted to the systemic study of all kinds of signs, including those of human language (linguistics).

Saussure's ideas influenced, among others, the group known as the Russian Formalists in the years just after his death. In the mid-1920s, the Prague Linguistic Circle also drew heavily upon his ideas. Both of these groups, in turn, influenced structuralism as it developed in France in the 1950s and 1960s, especially as exemplified by Roland Barthes.

## Russian Formalism and the Prague School

The thinkers broadly termed Russian Formalists flourished between 1915 to 1930. They comprised two separate but ideologically related groups, the Moscow Linguistic Circle (founded in 1915), mostly linguists, and the Petersburg Society for the Study of Poetic Language (Opojaz) (founded in 1916), mainly historians of literature. Various theorists were involved with these circles, but most relevant for our purposes was Roman Jakobson (1896-1982), a member of the Moscow group who moved to Czechoslovakia in 1920 and helped to found the Prague Linguistic Circle, heir to the Russian Formalist tradition.

Although the Russian Formalists disagreed on some points, they also shared some common ground. This included the belief that literature, especially poetry, was an entity in its own right, separate from external factors such as history, philosophy, psychology, economics, sociology, and so forth. All realms outside the formal structure of the work of art were minimized. Even the individual writer, especially if he spoke of mysticism and the unconscious, was given little importance. Instead, the author was seen as merging with the larger structure and momentum of the literary work.

The Russian Formalists wanted to probe the nature of literature, the elements that constituted it as an artistic phenomenon, responsible essentially to itself. Dynamically evolving technique and craft, rather than genius and inspiration, took priority. It was desirable for the materials of the writer to be liberated from their utilitarian (instrumental) function. Emphasis was placed on a series of devices that translated the author's material into an aesthetic whole, a unity that possessed a satisfying structure. The work was seen as having no "content" and needed no personalized characters who would convey a traditional narrative. Formal structure in the present (an echo of Saussure's synchronic emphasis) was in itself the reason for the work's existence.

Many, but not all, of the Russian Formalists' principles were carried on by the Prague Linguistic Circle, founded in 1926. Also influenced by Saussure, the Prague School (as it was called), together with the Russian Formalists, is now recognized as a major forerunner of modern structuralism. Jakobson, a key figure in the Prague group, who coined the word "structuralism" in 1929, is cited again and again by proponents of that approach, especially in the Paris of the 1960s and 1970s.

Members of the Prague Linguistic Circle, though certainly different from each other, cherished a set of unified views about literature and culture. Above all, they addressed sign systems, the essential core of semiotics. For these scholars, semiotic thinking was linked to and supported by language, and thus linguistic structure became central to their enterprise. The Prague School's overarching concern, then, was with aesthetic structures in literary works. This was not aesthetics for its own sake, in a closed system, as the Russian Formalists viewed the matter, but rather aesthetic character seen in relation to the work's reception by the reader, whose perceptions are not static, but variable and subject to change.

The Prague Circle also gave renewed attention to the author (denied by the Russian Formalists) as a maker of structures, though the author admittedly owed a relatively small debt to the reality around him or to past historical traditions. The Prague theorists, however, kept cultural life in focus, for they believed that a unified system of signs and structures belonged to a given society at any particular historical moment. Literary history became mainly a sequential development of formal devices or a changing aesthetic code.

The Prague Linguistic Circle went underground in 1939, when the Nazis closed the universities in Czechoslovakia. Jakobson and other members of the group fled the country, Jakobson settling in the United States in 1941 and remaining here principally as a teacher until his death in 1982. His influence in Western Europe and the United States seems to have been greater than any other member of the Russian Formalist group or Prague School. His ideas affected, among others, the anthropologist Claude Lévi-Strauss, a leading champion of structuralism in France, as well as the psychoanalyst Jacques Lacan, variously called a structuralist and a poststructuralist. In the meantime, the Prague Linguistic Circle was reconstituted after the war and operated during Czechoslovakia's democratic period (1945-48), before being declared un-Marxist by the Soviet-backed regime that took control of the country.

## Claude Lévi-Strauss

Claude Lévi-Strauss (b. 1908), an anthropologist, is viewed by many as the father of structuralism in its modern sense. Although he owed a considerable debt to Saussure (he was also influenced by other specialists, Roman Jakobson and N. S. Troubetskoy, who stressed the role of the unconscious), he expanded Saussure's ideas in a wide-ranging approach to problems in anthropology and the social sciences. For example, Lévi-Strauss studied all kinds of cultural behavior in so-called "primitive" societies — manners, kinship systems, dress, methods of cooking, and so on, as part of an integrated system, a total uniform "language" modeled after structural linguistics. The links to Saussure are obvious; but the main difference is that Lévi-Strauss dealt with all cultural phenomena, including social life, not merely spoken or written language.

One aspect of this larger cultural language that intrigued Lévi-Strauss was the telling of myths. He discovered, as Edith Kurzweil has observed, that "languages as well as myths of different cultures resembled each other and appeared to be structured in a similar fashion" (Kurzweil, 17). Following Saussure's *langue/parole* framework, Lévi-Strauss tried to discover the *langue* of each total cultural system as revealed through the specific usage of its *parole*. He found that he could account for some parts of the myth-making process only by referring to the unconscious mind not just of individuals, but also of entire cultures. Lévi-Strauss had admitted the influence of Sigmund Freud on his thinking and also came under the spell of the psychoanalyst Jacques Lacan, who in turn had been a structuralist. Thus, Lévi-Strauss fused a belief in the unconscious structuring capacity of the human mind with the more traditional intellectual logic of Saussure. Following Saussure, he saw meaning, to borrow John Storey's words, "as a result of the interplay between a process of similarity and difference" (Storey, 73).

In his exploration of the mind of "savages," Lévi-Strauss discovered that their thinking was different from that of those who lived in civilized nations. The nonliterate "savage" possessed another kind of logic, a mode of thinking that ordered the world according to the technique he called "bricolage." By this, Lévi-Strauss meant assembling information in a kind of improvised or patchwork manner, searching out analogies between disparate things rather than abiding by an overarching abstract framework. The principal realm of this kind of thought, Lévi-Strauss pointed out, is the relation of man to nature; the "primitive" man can say "I am a bear" and seem perfectly convincing, even logical, though his understanding of bears is very different from ours (Hawkes, 50).

To sum up: Lévi-Strauss ingeniously applied a linguistic model to his study of a whole range of "primitive" or "savage" cultures. In this work, he operated as a structuralist, discovering similarities (and differences) in the elements that make up the beliefs of different societies. This procedure enabled him to articulate these patterns and to conclude that patterns (or relationships) were repeated from one society to the next.

Lévi-Strauss thought he was being scientific in his studies, but, as his critics have pointed out, his science was frequently compromised by his personal intuitions and insights. His opponents also observed that he neglected the role of the individual and took an essentially ahistorical view of mankind, for, echoing Saussure, he believed that history, when it is recollected, becomes part of the present.

Lévi-Strauss was a pertinent model, especially from the mid 1950s to the late 1960s, for those who wished to see how structural linguistics could be applied to larger cultural and social issues. He showed, as well, how literary criticism could profit from his teachings, and he became a beacon for certain modern artists, like Jack Burnham, who wanted to apply structuralist insights in their own creative work. His name and ideas are not fashionable today, but French structuralism could not have developed as productively as it did without his example.

# CHAPTER 3

# FROM STRUCTURALISM TO POSTSTRUCTURALISM AND BEYOND

## Michel Foucault

Michel Foucault (1926-1984) was a man of many talents. He delved into philosophy, sociology, criminology, history of medicine, psychiatry, and cultural criticism; but he is best known as a historian of systems of thought (he held a chair in that subject, named by him, at the Collège de France, Paris). From structuralist beginnings (though he denied being a structuralist), he moved into a poststructural mode, his main (but not only) frame of reference for the rest of his life. He thus belongs in the company of Barthes, Derrida, Lacan, Lyotard, and other noted figures who became poststructuralists, and, like them, he carved out his own particular areas of study. His dominant concerns were the concept of power and the abnormal (criminals, the insane, sexual deviants, and so on).

Knowledge, Foucault believed, is intimately connected to power; those who wish to represent a certain kind of knowledge must have the necessary power to do so. Often an influential minority can seize this power and decide which version of truth or correctness will be followed by others. This goal, Foucault tells us, is achieved not by physical power, but primarily through language. In this belief, he reveals his allegiance to the structuralists.

Abnormal personalities intrigued Foucault because in deviation he was able to find a key to how various cultures identify normality and abnormality in terms of power. In a word, those who have the power can and will define what is "normal" in their own terms. But these defi-

38

nitions change from period to period, and thus the existence of any absolute final word on these matters is open to question. The only certain point is that people who are "normal" exercise the necessary power to hold sway over those who are "abnormal."

Within the societies that interested Foucault are found concentrations of power, sometimes hidden, but influential nonetheless. Channels of power, he observed, are used within institutions and social structures to control people so that sexual, political, and revolutionary action will be difficult, if not impossible. Although power is linked to ideologies, it is not connected in a linear, monolithic way. Power relations are, at times, unfocused or obscure, following an irregular pattern of give and take. However, systems or total institutions can repress individuals, even to the point of denying their freedom. Furthermore, human beings may not ever be able to take command of their language — an essential medium in Foucault's agenda of power revealed through discourse. Indeed, the concept of man is replaced by language, which seems to have a "mind" of its own. For Foucault, man as a concept becomes obsolete.

Foucault's concern was not with individuals but with changes in and connections between historical periods viewed structurally, that is, each one having a set of common beliefs and practices called "epistemes." Each episteme, in turn, embraces a series of "discourses," these being guidelines for any given epoch that include the specialized language and shared assumptions belonging to one discipline or another. There may be a multitude of discourses in any era, each affecting the other, and they may change over time. Although one discourse will not be more correct than another — there is no true or false — discourses have a kind of autonomous power to govern what may be said at a given time or place. Foucault believed that discourses structure our lives; individuals (authors, the "subject," etc.) do not structure the discourse.

Foucault employed a method that he called "archaeology," outlined in his book *The Archaeology of Knowledge* (1969), to delve beneath the surface, to probe the governing assumptions of earlier epochs. His search, however, was not for universal truths, grand totalizing theories, or the history of ideas, but for everchanging epistemes, themselves constructed of discursive codes that are mutable and even governed by unconscious factors. What distinguishes Foucault from conventional scholars is his view of diversity in the historical process: discourses may be numerous and individualized, with none claiming priority; the changes from one set of cultural assumptions to another may be sudden, not smooth. As Foucault said, archaeology "does not have a unifying but a diversifying effect" (Foucault, 160).

A sense of uncertainty came to play a greater role in Foucault's thought after he had read Friedrich Nietzsche's *Genealogy of Morals*. The ideas of the German philosopher encouraged Foucault to abandon his rather structured view of history in favor of a more irrational outlook, for which he borrowed Nietzsche's term "genealogy." This meant that the numerous branches we associate with a genealogical chart or tree have no logical destination; unlike the conventional image of a family's growth, these offshoots do not progress to an ever higher, better goal. Accident prevails over logic, and absolute truths, especially moral verities, cease to exist.

Although Foucault had briefly been a member of the Communist Party in the early 1950s and sympathized with the radical students who rioted in Paris in 1968, his writings have been judged to be politically noncommittal by activists on the Left. Indeed, Marshall Berman felt that in his texts Foucault offered an alibi to '60s people who went on in the '70s to experience a "sense of passivity and helplessness" (Berman, 35). Yet Foucault himself felt that political resistance was necessary and desirable. He saw his scholarly works as a way of making people aware of the social controls that govern their lives. As he said in 1971: "One must put 'in play,' show up, transform, and reverse the systems which quietly order us about" (Foucault in Fillingham, 151).

Foucault offered a perceptive look at the character of historical periods and the phenomena of the abnormal, past and present. But in this process, he spent much of his time tearing down totalizing intellectual and social theories that had prevailed in the past — especially those linked to the humanist views of the Enlightenment and to modernism in general (including Marxism and existentialism). Even Foucault's language, especially in his later writings, challenges logic and rational understanding: it can be poetic, obscure, and hard to fathom. As the historian Hayden White has observed: "There is no centre to Foucault's discourse. It is all surface — and intended to be so. For even more consistently than Nietzsche, Foucault resists the impulse to seek an origin or transcendental subject which would confer any specific meaning on human life. Foucault's discourse is wilfully superficial" (White, 82). Not only is the transcendental ego of the individual denied (toward the end of his life Foucault did admit that human agency had its place), history as a systematic, sequential account of society's progress is negated, and science and rationality are questioned because they serve capitalism and oppress the marginal elements in society.

In a sense, Foucault can best be defined in terms of his negative views, that is, what he did *not* believe in. Thus, in the shorthand of critical theory, he is anti-structural as well as post-structural; anti-humanist; and both anti-modern and postmodern.

## Roland Barthes

In the eyes of the educated public, Roland Barthes (1915-1980) appears to be the ultimate structuralist. He took the various strands of structuralist thinking (especially Saussure, Lévi-Strauss, the Russian Formalists, and others) and wove them into an engaging fabric that bridged structuralism and semiotics. Thanks to his sophisticated mind and his deft pen, he became the standard bearer for these ideas in the field of literary criticism, though he also ranged out into popular culture as well. Barthes stood as a bastion against literary existentialism and Marxist criticism and in the late 1960s and '70s became the ultimate culture hero. His name seemed to be on the lips of every French intellectual. American followers took a while to catch up with Barthes, but when they did, they echoed his ideas faithfully through the mid-1980s.

It is said that Barthes knew little or nothing of structuralism when he composed his first book, *Writing Degree Zero* (1953), a discourse on style and non-style. But not surprisingly, his keen interest in the workings of literary language led him to embrace the structural method, which he did in his book *Mythologies* (1957). There he showed how bourgeois "codes" are embedded in the mass media and are thus reinforced in the eyes of the consumer. In this volume, he set forth a method of establishing meanings (or values) that is based in part on Saussure. The Swiss theorist, we will recall, believed that the word for a particular object, for example a tree, designated that object but did not possess any of the qualities of a tree. This process and its result was called a linguistic sign. Barthes, however, thought this scheme was too limited because it merely consisted of a primary act of signifying. He added a second level of signification in which the already established signified (the tree) becomes a *new* signifier that points to a more elaborate signified, in this case the tree as an organic phenomenon that offers shelter and contributes to the beauty of nature. This more complex scheme, in turn, allowed Barthes to deal with what he called "myth"

42

(hence the title of his book, *Mythologies*). To Barthes, myth meant any kind of discourse belonging to "a second-order semiological system," to use his words.

Barthes placed structuralism on a more intellectual, even scientific, footing in *On Racine* (1963), a book in which he looked at Racine's plays from a totally new critical perspective. Abandoning biographical, aesthetic, sociopolitical, and psychological approaches — all had been done, but did not satisfy Barthes — he applied a method that weighed the texts in their own terms, dealing with internal relationships, which is to say, he followed a structural approach. Specifically, he employed what he called a "Racinian anthropology" (Hawkes, 111) through which he sought to reveal the plays' underlying psychological structures in systems of "oppositions" that come together to produce meaning. Barthes saw each play as a whole, "an autonomous entity of internal dependencies," to quote Michael Moriarty (Moriarty, 64). But he also related each play to the others in an overview of what Racine's theater was all about and, as Moriarty has observed, found himself "cutting across the boundaries between one text and another in the quest for the fundamental structures of an author's imagination" (ibid., 63).

All of this seemed quite radical to the French literary establishment. *On Racine* was vehemently attacked by Professor Raymond Picard of the Sorbonne in a bitter leaflet (1965) that accused Barthes of subverting the time-honored values of French literary criticism. Barthes countered with his own publication (1966) in which he defended his structuralist position. Debates among French intellectuals raged over this controversy. As a result, Barthes gained a place in the limelight, and his views ultimately triumphed.

Barthes' book *Elements of Semiology* (1964) is his most scientific and logical moment, the pinnacle of his interest in semiotic structuralism. Barthes' particular brand of semiology was heavily indebted to linguists, especially Saussure (earlier, Saussure had envisioned a science of signs, or semiology), but also the Russian Formalists and Lévi-Strauss. Under their influence, Barthes gave shape to a doctrine of structural semiology (or semiotics) that could be applied not only to the interpretation of literary works, but also to such mundane matters as clothing, food, furniture, and automobiles. His "binary" concepts of "Language and Speech," "Signifier and Signified," "Syntagm and System," and "Denotation and Connotation" became standard fare among like-minded intellectuals from the 1960s through the '80s and even later. He would abandon this stance later on, but for the moment it seemed that structural thinking was his key not only to language but also to a whole science of culture.

Barthes' ideas on language/speech (*langue/parole*) stem from Saussure, but he (Barthes) extended them, in the spirit of Lévi-Strauss, to cover social behavior as well as ideas of the collective unconscious and, indeed, "all systems of signs" (Barthes, 25). Like Saussure, too, he dwelt on the relation of the signifier and the signified, already part of his thinking in his earlier writings. But in *Elements of Semiology*, he reasserted his broader view of the sign, expanded and developed it, and explored additional complex ways in which a sign could point to expression and content.

In *Elements of Semiology* Barthes dealt with the two "axes" of language, first articulated by Saussure as the syntagmatic (horizontal) and the associative (vertical) and then adopted by Jakobson, following Saussure (who called the associative axis the paradigmatic; Barthes, in turn, named it the systematic plane). (Barthes, 58-59). The latter plane, sometimes also called the axis of combination, Barthes noted, has "a very close connection with 'the language' as a system, while the syntagm is nearer to speech" (Barthes, 59). Going one step further, Barthes, under Jakobson's influence, linked the syntagmatic plane with the metonymic and the paradigmatic plane with the metaphoric, forming another parallel set of oppositions. The first, the metonymic, according to Jakobson, belongs to such things as epic narratives and realist writing, while the second, the metamorphic, relates to Romantic and Symbolist works and the art of the Surrealists.

In the final section of his book, covering denotation and connotation, Barthes immerses himself in a maze of semiotic notions which are presented none too clearly — an irony because one of his professed goals was to promote logical certainties in language. To understand his concept of denotation and connotation, let us turn first to the standard definitions, then come back to Barthes. The denotation of a word or linguistic unit is the specific thing or person (that is, in effect, its primary dictionary meaning). The connotation of a word or phrase refers to its emotional significance or the associations it calls up. To use an example cited by M. H. Abrams: "Home denotes the house where one lives, but connotes privacy, intimacy, and coziness" (Abrams, 35).

For Barthes, the linguistic signifier's literal reference to the signified operates on the plane of denotation. This "first" system, in turn, becomes "the plane of expression, or signifier" (or a "sign" that is a signifier of connotation) of a new system, a second system which is the plane of connotation. With this procedure, metalanguage is brought into play. (Metalanguage is generally defined as a higher-level language that is used to describe language [or an object-language]. For example, linguistics itself is such a language.) Metalanguage, in turn, can become the object-language of another metalanguage and so on, indefinitely.

Analysis of the codes in clothing became the subject of his next major book, *The Fashion System* (1967), which took as its subject the language used in contemporary fashion magazines. His approach in this work "of nearly unbearable tedium" (Jackson, 145) is insistently semiotic, drawing largely on the theories he outlined in *Elements of Semiology*. But now he applies them to a specific subject from the world of popular culture. Two systems — the rhetorical system and the "vestimentary" code — serve as the basis for his arguments. The former, being linguistic, consists of fashion writing as a signifier and also as a signified (that is, an ideology) which involves the fashion world. The vestimentary code, in turn, relates to the actual appearance of clothing — blouses, collars, gowns, and so on. Barthes relied on a strict linguistic model involving phrase-structure trees to explain how outfits became fashionable. Such garb is different from the usual daily clothing and is governed by a codified, stable language of fashion, which is, as Jack Burnham tells us, "not only evident but predictable." Haute couture Barthes sees "as a central concern of Semiology, embodying descriptions of intelligence, sensibility, direction, and opinion within society's tastemaking strata" (Burnham, 27).

*Elements of Semiology* and *The Fashion System* represent the pinnacle of Barthes' most structural or semiotic phase. During this time he believed in the ultimate power of one-to-one linguistic relationships, orderly concepts that could be diagrammed and rationally explained. Much of what he studied reflected back on itself, that is, operated as a closed system in which the structure of language became a self-contained goal. Because of this, some even viewed Barthes negatively as a formalist. However, he took pains to point out that his semiotic systems, based on language, also echoed social and cultural assumptions in the real world. As Barthes argued in *Elements of Semiology*, the signifieds he dealt with — signifieds of connotation — have a "very close communication with culture, knowledge, and history, and it is through them, so to speak, that the environmental world invades the system" (Barthes, 91-92). Although Barthes undoubtedly believed what he was saying, those who have closely studied his structuralist writings find that they feed upon themselves, which is to say, they deal with linguistic relationships within a kind of closed scientific system, almost like a series of algebraic formulae.

All of this changed in Barthes' next book, *S/Z* (1970), an analysis of a short story by Balzac. In this volume, structuralism is challenged and overcome by poststructuralist ideas. Although Barthes at first tips his hat to structuralism by setting up five "codes" which are used to draw inferences, and hence meaning, from Balzac's story, he sidesteps any fixed interpretation, indeed backs away from the fruits of "theory." Of increasing interest to Barthes is the fluid way texts work in relation to codes (an idea he gleaned from Julia Kristeva), coming together in a kind of woven fabric or network. This notion of "textuality" denies the power and uniqueness of the individual writer (or subject); and brings about the death of the author, whose influence, he says, ought to give way to a dominant textual interplay of codes. Instead of the author, the *reader* is placed at center stage. This idea upsets the orderly hierarchies of literary experience and, in a poststructural sense, disorients the inquiring public. That is not all. Under Jacques Derrida's influence, Barthes threatened the controlled, predictable structuralism (much of it of Barthes' own making) he had presented in *S/Z* by offering a series of intellectual insider jokes; denying that a text has a fixed, single meaning; and failing to address the unitary structure of Balzac's story. These "subversive" traits are part and parcel of his new poststructural outlook.

From this point to 1980, the year of his death, Barthes' writing grew to be more and more poststructural in character. Particularly indebted to poststructuralism was the contrast he drew between the "readerly" (*lisible*) and "writerly" (*scriptible*), outlined in *S/Z* and developed in his book *The Pleasure of the Text* (1973). While the traditional readerly text dealt transparently and matter-of-factly with things in the real world, posing no challenges, Barthes' writerly text called attention to itself as a literary phenomenon. He thus turned away from the older view that texts have fixed meanings passively absorbed by the audience. The writerly text involves an approach not only to the making of texts but also to the way in which they are absorbed by the public: an approach that involves the reader's (the subject's) shifting, changing involvement with the text, depending on his or her own values and experiences. (The effects of these kinds of writing are, to use Barthes' terms, *plaisir* [relaxed enjoyment], in the first instance, and *jouissance* [a kind of orgasmic bliss or sudden delight] in the second case.) Barthes finally appears to have rediscovered the human senses.

Not only the readers' (also Barthes') pleasure in experiencing texts but also their delight in the body and eroticism invade Barthes' writings of the early 1970s (*Empire of Signs*, 1970; *Sade/Fourier/Loyola*, 1971). Even the self — his own — became the topic of one of his last works, an autobiographical essay, *Roland Barthes by Roland Barthes* (1975). This uncovered facets of the author that his earlier structuralism had concealed, revealing a human being who possessed a vibrant self — a responsive body that could interact with signs and a mind that intuitively juggled fragments and impressions. This increasingly personal Barthes found his fullest expression in *Camera Lucida* (1980), published in the year of his death. In that work, his sensitive personal response to the medium of photography triumphed over structuralism and semiotics. The strength of the book lies in the author's intuitive poetic language, his willingness to look lovingly at the idiosyncracies of the illusionary vocabulary of the photographic image.

In the last decade of his life, Barthes nurtured literary ambitions of his own. He published several novels that enjoyed some success; but in the last analysis he was at his best in writing critical essays. In these, his prose became more and more suggestive and evocative, as if to indicate that there could be no closure, no resolution in the world of ideas. Dogma was anathema to Barthes, and he sidestepped anything that might be called ideology. In this connection, his language carried an inevitable "political" aura; although removed from worldly activism himself, he believed that showing the nature and influence of language was somehow a political act. His later writings, particularly, become a verbal model of how language could undermine authority and, by extension, dislocate any regulatory pattern of thought. In taking this position, he indulged in a kind of vague, metaphorical writing, suggestive and impressionistic, difficult to pin down. The result is thoroughly post-structural.

## Jacques Derrida

Some have considered Jacques Derrida (b. 1930) a philosopher, while others have called him a cultural theorist or a literary critic. Whatever label is applied to him, he possesses an enormously influential and challenging mind, and he has upset a wide range of accepted literary, philosophical, and cultural beliefs. He has done this mostly as the standard-bearer for the approach called deconstruction, not a theory or a method but rather a strategy or practice. As with his fellow thinkers who held similar interests or fell under his influence, Derrida's writing can be obtuse and suggestive rather than easily accessible. No matter, his ideas have had a magnetic appeal for many (but not all) intellectuals, and he has become a prophet in his own time.

Unlike Barthes, who went through several gradual stages or changes in his thinking, discovering himself along the way, Derrida made a focused, head-on attack on a variety of clearly defined problems. He did this in the late 1960s and early 1970s in books such as *Of Grammatology* (1967), *Writing and Difference* (1967), *Speech and Phenomena* (1967), *Margins of Philosophy* (1972), and *Dissemination* (1972). All of these demonstrate how his close reading of texts from a variety of fields —literature, philosophy, psychoanalysis, linguistics, and anthropology — can produce a new and disorienting perspective. Derrida's deconstructive approach is a way of looking at and reading a text that not only deconstructs that piece of writing but also the whole world view that gave rise to it. And part of that (older) world view is structuralism, which he challenges in any number of ways. The structuralists, we will recall, believed that a larger set of linguistic principles, like the rules of chess, governed the formation of language and that individual speech events (*parole*) were worked out within the system with a certain amount of free choice and flexibility. The structural view was essentially logical, predictable, and remote from history, social issues, and individual effort.

Derrida started, under Freud's influence, by dissolving the practice of producing meaning through signs. He thinks there cannot be a clear cause-and-effect relationship between signifier and signified in a text because the reader's presuppositions and intuitions, even unconscious insights, may affect the way meaning is experienced. Moreover, the author apparently enjoys little control over the text because, in Derrida's opinion, he is subordinated to the governing rhetorical conventions (tropes) of the language available to him, a language that has a life of its own. The cultural landscape could thus be viewed as a series of texts that interact with each other — hence the term "intertextuality," prized not only by Derrida but also by Roland Barthes when he came under Derrida's influence.

Derrida also mounted a campaign against the established dualities in Western philosophy (and which survive in the structural thinking of Saussure and Lévi-Strauss) that took the form of binary pairs like nature/culture, health/disease, male/female, truth/error, speech/writing, and so on. In these, the first term is the privileged one and the second belongs to the "margin," following the analogy of the marginal comments surrounding the main text on a printed page. For Derrida, what takes place in the margins may be just as revealing as the principal text. Thus, he thinks, priority may be reshuffled in a binary pair. There is no reason why, in Derrida's view, the lesser term should not be awarded greater prominence. To maintain the newly created reversal, Derrida reinscribes or inserts, as Robert Con Davis, explains, "the newly inferior term [male] within the class of the newly superior term [female]" (Davis, 410). This step dissolves outmoded polar opposites, a good thing, for these are relics of a system of hierarchial ranking that has unjustly permeated Western civilization.

Derrida's most telling move was to cast his lot with the discredited second half of the binary pair of speech/writing. The spoken word, he thinks, has improperly dominated the annals of philosophy from Plato to Hegel and from Rousseau to the semiotics of Saussure. This view, called "logocentric" (focus on the "word," a kind of foundational or original truth) or "phonocentric" (speech as a carrier of stable truths, superior to writing), gives priority to the word as the "transcendental signified." The spoken word in this sense is the vehicle for some essential, authentic truth, a metaphysical reality above and beyond the signifying language itself — and all of this is produced and controlled by a willful, masterful author. "Presence" is the trait Derrida associates with this world view: a kind of stable, permanent center served by an authoritarian voice.

Writing, the other side of the equation, stresses not a "metaphysics of presence" but the willingness to challenge time-honored priorities or rankings. The character of writing, Derrida thinks, is subversive, fluid, an experience, a trace that can live without the assertive evidence of an author's presence. By its very nature, writing is set free from the authority of speech. As Christopher Norris put it, "Writing is condemned to circulate endlessly from reader to reader, the best of whom can never be sure that they have understood the author's original intent. Its effect is to 'disseminate' meaning to a point where the authority of origins is pushed out of sight by the play of a henceforth limitless interpretative freedom" (Norris, 8).

Derrida's special way of thinking is epitomized by his ideas on "difference." Saussure, we will recall, used linguistic differences as a way of distinguishing between sounds; this is how word-meanings were created. Derrida, too, works with the notion of difference, but in a much more complex and multilayered way, ultimately rejecting Saussure. For Derrida, there is a clever play on words when he places the French nouns "différence" and "différance" side-by-side as a way of defining the dual character of the sign. The root verb for each is *différer* (= to differ), and the two nouns (*différence* and *différance*) made from that verb sound alike. But their meanings are not the same. *Différence* means difference or differentiation, while *différance* means deferral, holding back.

Derrida says *différence/différance* works in two overlapping ways. In the first instance, it refers to the manner in which Saussure found that meaning was formed; but in the second case, it points to an opposite view: that exact meaning is always deferred. That is, we cannot fully grasp any meaning (or signified) presented to us by language. Although the context of a verbal expression may offer some help in the interpretation of language, permanent meanings often escape the reader, even to a point of endless delay or deferral. There is, in other words, something that always escapes language, the result of an impasse called an "aporia."

In a larger sense, this notion of deferral governed Derrida's cautious interpretation of texts, whether literary or some other kind of cultural artifact, which can also be a text. He had come to distrust absolutes in the Western tradition, like truth and authorship. He agreed that such concepts existed, but he viewed them as being subject to change over time rather than permanent "essences" that can be revealed to the rational mind. He goes so far as to say that we cannot establish meaning in any human construction or text. Rational knowledge and even history become hard to grasp, "aleatory," or randomly unpredictable. Thus, for Derrida the idea of sequence, both present and past, is invalid.

Derrida initiated deconstruction and is (or was) its prime exponent. But he seemed reluctant to step forward as the parent of a movement based on his ideas. He sees deconstruction as a difficult and demanding approach to texts that must be pursued by a devoted reader. He admits, moreover, that even he cannot give an ironclad definition of deconstruction and insists that it is a way of reading, not a theory or a method. All of this is odd, because Derrida's admirers have worshiped him as an intellectual deity and have followed him as the principal leader in literary criticism and philosophy that flourished in the United States.

Especially energetic in building on Derrida's ideas were the deconstructive literary critics and theorists Paul de Man, J. Hillis Miller, Harold Bloom (for a time), and Geoffrey Hartman, who dominated the Yale English department in the early 1980s. Barbara Johnson and Jonathan Culler also followed suit. These ideas were defined in the arts, especially in the United States and England, by a complex network of art critics and historians associated with universities, museums, and art journals. Artists themselves tended to shy away from deconstruction, but architects embraced the idea more quickly, and some architectural writers jumped on the bandwagon.

Deconstruction, it should be stated — following Derrida — is less a philosophical stance than "a way of thinking about and reading texts," as Stephen Connor put it (Connor, 49). In a sense, everything can be viewed as a text (or cultural artifact), and these texts interact one with another, almost as if they had a life of their own. The "author," as Derrida and his colleagues (especially Barthes) tell us, is dead. While this pronouncement may be extreme, it is safe to say that the deconstructionists believe the rhetorical habits of any given milieu take priority over the author's personal intent. And we find in Derrida and Barthes, especially, the notion that the reader's (and also the critic's) interaction with the text helps to produce meaning. Because the mental and emotional activity of the reader changes from person to person, and also according to the time when the reader lives, there can be no single correct interpretation of any text. Moreover, texts seem to have no hope of projecting any definitive, coherent meaning because deconstructive strategies of criticism continually explore the margins, not the center, to find the exceptions, not the rule. Traditional emphasis on the "center," deconstructionists believe, has unjustly marginalized certain genders and classes of people. Such thinkers deal with signifiers without necessarily needing them to refer to the real world (nature) or to some transcendental truth beyond the text. Reference to a network of other texts (intertextuality) takes priority.

If they do not delve systematically into the past, deconstructionists do break down the rigid barriers that separate the intellectual territory and social institutions they address, much as Foucault had done in his writings in the 1960s. This procedure encourages critics to seek connections between their discipline and other domains, links to other arts and sciences. This dissolving of divisions also applies to the different media of the arts; painting and sculpture, for example, are no longer separated from one another, and there is an accompanying breakdown of the differences between fine and popular art. Following Derrida, the division between male and female may be bridged, as well as the gap between all previously privileged and marginalized terms.

## Jacques Lacan

Jacques Lacan (1901-1980) worked as a psychiatrist, then as a psychoanalyst, but he was also well versed in philosophy, linguistics, and anthropology. Although much of the established psychoanalytic community (particularly in the United States) rejected Lacan because of his unconventional ideas, he attracted a circle of admirers within French psychiatric circles and, among other places, in the fields of literary criticism, cultural studies, and film theory. Foucault, Barthes, and Derrida, just to name a few key figures, fell under his influence. But it is hard to fit Lacan neatly into the structural-poststructural continuum with which these figures are associated. For example, Lacan's fascination with the unconscious mind keeps him from falling into the structuralist camp. Yet he followed structural models for his appraisal of the human mind, a step that would seem to diminish his ties with postmodernism. Still, he does resemble the poststructuralists in believing that the self is decentered; that signifiers can be slippery and lead merely to other signifiers; and that it may thus be hard to capture exact meanings. Lacan's own prose at his most suggestive moments is often enigmatic and borders on the poetic, even at times becoming incomprehensible.

Lacan admired, above all, the theories of Sigmund Freud, especially his emphasis on the unconscious mind. In fact, Lacan championed Freud during a time when the Viennese analyst was out of fashion. Like Freud, Lacan perceived a tension between the conscious and unconscious parts of the mind, the latter, in his view, carrying out a dialogue with the conscious mind but being essentially unknowable or alien. But whereas Freud believed that psychotherapy would eventually lead to a rational wholeness and unity in the human personality, Lacan thought such a goal was unattainable because of an unresolved psychic division stemming from what Lacan called the "mirror stage" in early childhood. This was one of the steps in the unfolding of the Oedipal complex (borrowed from Freud) and a cornerstone in Lacan's thinking.

After an "imaginary" or pre-Oedipal phase, where the child is at one with the mother, he sees himself in a mirror and realizes that it is his own image. This initial preverbal and impressionistic encounter produces a powerful impact on the youngster. It is here that the subject perceives himself in a narcissistic fashion; and, engaging the libido, he also finds that he exists as an ego, or "I," separate from the "other," whether other persons or some aspect of the self revealed in the mirror. This first reaction brings about a tension or split that involves competition with the "other" or "others," thus evoking hostility or aggressiveness. Lacan points out that the mirror stage initiates various misperceptions (*méconnaissances*) on the part of the subject, who may cling to the illusion that his ego is stable and unified. After this stage, however, the self, troubled by a perpetual unfulfilled "lack" or desire, focuses, Lacan says, on the unattainable figure of the mother.

The Oedipal myth unfolds when the child realizes that the father — the Law and a mythic being — is in the picture and that he (the child) is thus prevented from possessing the mother. The child recognizes this situation; and his own desire, laden with guilt, is thus repressed and hidden away in the unconscious mind. This step, however, leads to the youngster's socially appropriate acceptance of social norms through identification with the father, symbolized by the power of the phallus, what Lacan calls the primary signifier (women are relegated to a secondary position in this system). Language helps the child merge with society, language being discovered at the same time that he begins to recognize sexual differences.

Lacan delved into linguistic structuralism, especially Saussure, Jakobson, and Lévi-Strauss, in order to develop and expand his own interpretation of the Freudian unconscious. He was well aware of Saussure's notion of the signifier and signified, but Lacan's approach was less rigid than that of Saussure, for the French psychoanalyst believed that signifiers could carry varied messages, depending on their position in the world of other signifiers. He also appropriated Jakobson's idea of the two basic axes of language that revolve around metaphor (word-for-word substitution) and metonymy (word-to-word displacement). These concepts, Lacan believed, constituted the grammar of the unconscious, as well as of speech. The psychoanalyst, in turn, must listen to the flow of the patient's spoken words as well as his dreams, as Freud did, but pay special attention to the role of metaphor and metonymy in probing the governing concerns of the unconscious — which for him are "lack" or repressed desire.

For Lacan, all of language was metaphorical, thanks to the slipperiness of the unconscious mind. There could be no simple linear bond between the signifier and signified. Unfulfilled desire could thus be symbolized by an unending chain of signifiers, each leading to another and another. Lacan said the unconscious is "structured like a language" (Groden and Kreiswirth, 452). This idea can also be turned around to say that the language we use is like the unconscious — metaphorical, suggestive, and hard to pin down. Lacan's own prose typifies this very mode of thinking: it represents a hazy reality, rich in the mystery of the unconscious and alien to Saussure's stable way of linking signifiers to the signified. It is no wonder that reading Lacan can be a frustrating experience.

The troubling quality of Lacan's verbiage is a paradox because he sincerely wished to make his brand of psychoanalysis understood by the public. To that end, near the end of his life in 1981, he offered public lectures and television shows on the subject. A revolutionary spirit, he did not conceal his dislike for the traditional voices in the field of psychiatry and shook the discipline to its foundations. This radical stance, and the content of his teachings, caught on, particularly among the rebels who participated in the 1968 uprisings in Paris. As Madan Sarup observed, there was a feeling among "many students and workers that a liberated politics could only emerge from liberated interpersonal relationships, and there was an explosion of interest in Lacanian psycho-analysis" (Sarup, 6). It is worth noting, too, that Lacan and his followers took to the streets in 1968 and supported the radical cause. Generally, though, he was not an activist, preferring, like his French poststructuralist colleagues, to create new patterns in the realm of the mind, models that might alter the thinking and values of a sympathetic audience.

## Jean-François Lyotard

Like his other colleagues in the world of French critical theory, Jean-François Lyotard (1924-1998) does not fit neatly into any single discipline. He is principally a philosopher, but he also addresses questions of politics, economics, ethics, aesthetics, and criticism. His name, though, is most closely associated with the broad interdisciplinary concept of postmodernism, the subject of the book *The Postmodern Condition: A Report on Knowledge* (1979) which has made his reputation. Although he works with language, as Derrida, Barthes, and Lacan did, he is suspicious of "theory"; Lyotard is more comfortable in his engagement with real situations in the world, including the experience of art. For this reason, he can be more interesting to read than the other theorists just mentioned. His way of expressing himself, however, is at times just as ambiguous and confusing as theirs.

In his early thought, Lyotard fell under the influence of Edmund Husserl's phenomenology, a fitting launchpad (because it stressed individual experience) for Lyotard's distrust of "theory." Although the young Lyotard was a political activist on the Left, he broke from Marxist ideas, perhaps because they lent themselves too easily to system or "theory." For a time, the teachings of Freud attracted him, but even Freud fell out of favor as the Frenchman began to assemble his ideas on postmodernism. These notions did not spring fully formed onto the pages of *The Postmodern Condition,* but rather emerged bit by bit in what Steven Best and Douglas Kellner have called his protopostmodern phase (Best and Kellner, 152).

In the decade of the 1970s, Lyotard had come under the influence of Nietzsche, who steered him away from reason toward a kind of emotional state in which vital life-energies flowed freely. One of Lyotard's favorite concepts was "desire," a source of human creativity — this being a Freudian notion linked to the unconscious or the instincts but interpreted by Lyotard in his own personal way. Desire expresses itself through art and what Lyotard calls the "figure," a term that he contrasts with "discourse." He frowns on the latter because it is regulatory, literal, or word-oriented. By contrast, the figural favors "art," which is to say, forms of expression that stress sensation and metaphor, that are full of energy and at times irrational. Vision in this scheme is given desired priority over mind. Not surprisingly, Lyotard at this point attacks semiotic theories that stress the regulation of thought through structured language. Even in his own writing, as Best and Kellner point out, Lyotard "deconstructs" logical hegemonic discourses, preferring poetic, ambiguous language that is figural, a kind of painting with words (ibid.).

As of the mid-1970s, Lyotard moved away from the metaphysics of desire and a concern with aesthetics to the power of language. Within that realm — writing and speaking — he questioned and challenged all varieties of entrenched theories, universal truths, and comprehensive historical narratives (metanarratives), including Marxism, Freudianism, and the theory of the Enlightenment. Instead, he wanted to encourage marginalized or minority voices speaking in smaller narratives.

All of this is a preamble to Lyotard's best known and most influential book, *The Postmodern Condition: A Report on Knowledge* (1979), the English translation of which (1984) also includes his 1982 essay, "Answering The Question: What is Postmodernism?" In this volume he echoes some of his older ideas and develops new ones. Oddly, it is not a fully argued or comprehensive account of postmodernism, a subject already taken up by others by the time his book and accompanying essay were written. Thus, it should be viewed as one current in the ongoing stream of debates about postmodernism, not the definitive statement. That said, let us look at Lyotard's ideas on the subject.

His 1979 book deals, as the subtitle tells us, with the nature of knowledge, including, especially, scientific knowledge in advanced societies. Lyotard links this knowledge, together with technology, to social and political forces — capitalism, industrialism, state power, and the like

— both from the "modern" and the "postmodern" points of view. He says he is using the word "modern" to "designate any science that legitimates itself with reference to a metadiscourse . . . making an explicit appeal to some grand narrative" (quoted in Rose, 55). In this scheme, modern scientific knowledge is the culprit, for science belongs to an objective, regulated method of looking at the world and allies itself with the efficiencies of capitalism and the resulting domination of nature by this complex of forces. The postmodern, Lyotard says, relates to "the condition of knowledge in the most highly developed societies" (Lyotard, xxiii) and adds his often quoted but perhaps imperfectly understood definition of the postmodern as "incredulity toward metanarratives" (ibid., xxiv). Metanarratives are equated in his writings with the "grand narrative" just mentioned, including "metaphysical philosophy and the university institution which in the past relied on it" (ibid.). The post-industrial age, too, is an expression of postmodernism, as are the larger cultural issues of what he believes is a new era, replacing the modern. (Lyotard, however, places no emphasis on cultural matters in his 1979 text.) More than anything else, in Lyotard's view, the new (postmodern) science dismantles the hegemonic power of modern scientific discourse. As he says: "Postmodern science — by concerning itself with such things as undecidables, the limits of precise control, conflicts characterized by incomplete information, '*fracta*,' catastrophes, and pragmatic paradoxes — is theorizing its own evolution as discontinuous, catastrophic, nonrectifiable, and paradoxical" (ibid., 60). In addition, the modern goal of efficient performance is replaced by paralogy. This term, borrowed from the philosophical concept of going against logical truths or formulae, perfectly matched Lyotard's postmodern notion of science. Instead of being concerned with metanarratives, that science addressed local or molecular issues and worked in the realm of imagination, indeterminacy, and the unknown. As Lyotard said: "The little narrative remains the quintessential form of imaginative invention, most particularly in science" (ibid.).

Even language becomes an ally in helping Lyotard oppose older "modern," authoritarian, pragmatic modes of verbal expression, and he linguistically tries to deconstruct any schemes or institutions that smack of the totalitarian. The assuredness of semiotics, with its predictable way of communicating messages, repelled Lyotard; instead, he preferred "the flexible networks of language games," an idea based on Ludwig Wittgenstein, in which the rules are like those governing the moves in chess (ibid., 10). This should not suggest any rigidity or concession to practical speech. To the contrary, the give-and-take between speakers can be unpredictable and game-like, reflecting the quest for pleasure "in the endless invention of turns of phrase, of words and meanings, the process behind the evolution that the language on the level of *parole*" (ibid.). This practice stands in opposition to "accepted language" and offers, moreover, the chance of creating fluid social bonds. As I said earlier, Lyotard's book on postmodernism is not at all comprehensive. It is confined to postmodern patterns in the scientific-technical domain, without excluding social practices, but does not deal with broader artistic and cultural issues. These, however, were addressed in Lyotard's 1982 essay, "Answering the Question: What is Postmodernism?", though in a curiously personal, erratic way.

Lyotard defines the modern in art as an aesthetic of the "sublime," the presentation of the "unpresentable" — something "which can neither be seen nor made visible" (ibid., 78). He sees abstraction, a "withdrawal of the real" (ibid., 79), as inevitable and the artist's experiments and self-conscious sense of being in the avant-garde a means to this end.

Lyotard explains postmodernism, in turn, in an erratic, almost impressionist fashion. Postmodern artists, he finds, abandon artistic experiments, turn once again to the public, and seek "identity" and "security" (ibid., 73). The avant-garde dissolves in the face of an art that refers in varying degrees to "reality," often through references to the academic past. Eclecticism prevails in postmodernism, for one can borrow retrospectively from any style, and it matters little whether the language of art reflects good taste. So many possibilities are open that "anything goes" (ibid., 76), especially the once despised human subject and even kitsch.

In his summary of the postmodern, Lyotard erects a confusing framework that gives priority, in a curious way, to modernism. After speaking of the way each generation of modern artists may challenge the previous ones (Picasso and Braque, for example, attacked Cézanne), he asserts that the postmodern is part of the modern. To use his words, "A work can become modern only if it is first postmodern. Postmodernism thus understood is not modernism at its end, but in the nascent state, this state is constant" (ibid., 79). Lyotard goes on to explain (or try to) that the postmodern is tied to the notion of the unpresentable that typifies the modern. The postmodern artist or writer, he says, is even a philosopher, for his products are not "governed by preestablished rules, and they cannot be judged according to a determining judgement, by applying familiar categories to the text or to the work" (ibid., 81). Although the creative artist works without rules, he will "formulate the rules of what will have been done." Hence, the artistic product will be like an "event" (ibid.).

Lyotard's logic becomes even more slippery in his concluding remarks. He ultimately opts for that which "cannot be presented" (ibid.), sidestepping the idea of the "reconciliation between language games" toward a "real unity" (ibid.), a state that would lead to "terror." Lyotard said he had enough of that and thus once again declares war on "totality." (ibid., 82). "Let us," he says, "be witness to the unpresentable." (ibid.).

Lyotard maintains an odd place in the world of French theory. He was a widely published and respected intellect, yet he seems to have capitalized on a fairly limited number of ideas, which he repeated in different ways. Even his views on postmodernism, the subject for which he is best known, ironically appear unoriginal and at times derivative. It is worth noting that, while Lyotard was an esteemed contemporary of Foucault, Barthes, Derrida, and Lacan, his writings are often omitted from poststructural anthologies. Too, his name appears far less often than theirs in the debates on deconstruction and poststructuralism, a testament to his diminished position in the world of critical theory.

# Jean Baudrillard

Revered by many intellectuals, artists, and critics, the French sociologist Jean Baudrillard (b. 1929) is a leading guru of postmodernity. Compared to Lyotard, who also claimed to be a pioneer in this area, he is emphatically negative, an apostle of dehumanization and media overload who speaks of the thorough and total destruction of modernist values in the latter half of the 1980s. Today, the teachings of his fellow French theorists Foucault, Derrida, and Lacan — with whom he is often grouped — seem oddly irrelevant and out of date. While Baudrillard shares the poststructural orientation of these thinkers, he surpasses them in articulating a set of basic attitudes that separate modernism from the postmodern.

Although Baudrillard sees the modern-postmodern shift in terms of a change in the capitalist system — a move from the industrial to the postindustrial — his approach goes far beyond the economic. Influenced by semiotics and the writings of the Canadian theorist Marshall McLuhan on the media, he regards the onset of the postmodern as a crucial break in people's way of processing of signs and symbols. He points out that industrial capitalism, which is part and parcel of modernism, deals with the exchange of material commodities, a system based on the power of human labor. (Marx's opposition to capitalism and his drive for reform and emancipation — the other side of the modernist coin — is as irrelevant in postmodern times as is industrial capitalism itself.)

Baudrillard says people are no longer authentic, self-determined seekers after absolute values but rather function as an anonymous mass society that expresses itself through the survey, by means of public opinion polls. The electronic media, especially television, encourage social conformity. As Barry Smart points out, laborers, instead of being alienated (a state that troubled Marx), merge uncritically into their jobs, willingly taking up preordained social roles (Smart, 126). An endless bombardment of commercial messages from the mass media, again especially television, makes producers into unthinking consumers.

Postmodern people, Baudrillard argues, have moved from making material things to generating information, a shift to an abstract world of communication. Today, a new reality has taken over, one that is "unreal" by earlier standards because it is based on the simulacrum, or the sham or false: a reproduction of the real, not the real itself. In this scheme of things, the simulacrum has come to be more central than the object it signifies. Or to use Baudrillard's own analogy, the map is more pertinent than the territory it represents; indeed the map, the simulation, is now the real (Baudrillard, 2). The real, in Baudrillard's words, "is produced from miniaturized units, from matrices, memory banks and command modules." And with these methods, the new reality can be "reproduced an indefinite number of times" (ibid., 3). What we concern ourselves with is a series of reproductions of reality; as he says, "The real is not only what can be reproduced but that *which is always already reproduced,*" or the "hyperreal" (ibid., 146). It follows that there will no longer be any difference between an original (with an "aura") and a copy; and thus unending repetition becomes a hallmark of our postmodern era. Originality is impossible because everything, it seems, has already been done.

Modernist rationality, purpose, and linear thinking give way, in Baudrillard's view, to a nonrational world of fragments. Things are seen no longer as wholes, but as fleeting images, not linked in any logical fashion. Montage — disparate pieces thrown together — is a dominant postmodern mode of presentation. Even history is seen in fragments; as John Storey observes, its only value is a nostalgic escape back into a world more "real" than one filled with meaningless simulacra (Storey, 165).

Baudrillard is, in a sense, the heir of Walter Benjamin, as well as Marshall McLuhan. Benjamin spoke of the loss of "aura" of the original work of art in "an age of mechanical reproduction," to quote from the title of his best known essay (discussed earlier). He worried, too, about the effects of the mass media on the working classes, fearing that alien and controlling ideologies could be transmitted through this means, yet he also flirted with the positive effects of popular culture. McLuhan, who reached the height of his influence in the 1960s and 1970s, also addressed the question of mass communication, principally television, the dominant issue of his own time. For McLuhan, it was not the content of the message carried by television that counted. More important was the medium's perceptual makeup, or structure, and the way in which that struck its observers. Entire modes of thinking and feeling were altered by what was then a new visual mode of communication, one that had decisively challenged and displaced the older dominant print medium. Like McLuhan, Baudrillard concerned himself not with a given "content" presented to the spectator through one medium or another but rather with the way the very character of the medium itself alters our perceptions.

A tone of defeat and hopelessness permeates Baudrillard's definition of postmodernism. The universe of signs, without referents in the real world, leads us to an artificial reality that has to do with deception, montage, and the reading of our environment as a series of signs or scripts. For actual guilt, anguish and death, we substitute the *signs* for guilt, anguish, and death. He finds a kind of "nonintentional parody" hovering over everything, with simulations of real objects and experiences rather than these things in themselves being the material of our present culture (Baudrillard, 150). If we live in the domain of the "hyperreal," then we can only manipulate signs and codes, not actual events, political or otherwise, for we no longer have any connection with them. As John Storey points out, Baudrillard shares with Lyotard, the other leading French spokesman for postmodernism, a belief that the old tangible certainties (metanarratives) associated with modernism are gone forever

(Storey, 165). In Baudrillard, moreover, we do not find the usual leftist attacks on capitalism, and this is simply because the modernist issues of material production and labor have dissolved and have become unthreatening "signs." Capitalism has taken a new postmodern form — post-industrial, global, or neo-capitalist.

Perhaps more than any other theorist since World War II, Jean Baudrillard has influenced the direction of painting and photography. A whole movement, Simulationism, with a Baudrillard-like name and credo, flourished in the mid-to late 1980s. Similarly, a closely related group of artists who drew heavily upon appropriation also echoed Baudrillard's ideas; and even outside these circles, he was much talked about as cult figure and catalyst. Some, however, thought he was merely a creature of fashion. Michael Starenko called him in 1984 "the current dandy of new wave nihilism" and attacked his jargon-laced allusive writing as "poststructuralist science fiction" (*Afterimage*, January 1984, 14.). Yet whatever criticisms Baudrillard may have evoked, he was responsible for one of the main intellectual currents in 1980s culture.

# CHAPTER 4

# POSTSTRUCTURALISM
# AND POSTMODERNISM

## Poststructuralism

Deconstruction, as we have seen, is the brain-child of Jacques Derrida. It is a means of examining and interrogating texts and, more broadly, a philosophical view about how language works — or doesn't work. We might think of deconstruction as a Derridean tool, occasionally borrowed and used by others, that influences poststructuralism and helps make it possible. The goals of poststructuralism, though, become a bit broader in the hands of other practitioners such as Foucault, Barthes, Lacan, and of course Derrida himself. (Lyotard and Baudrillard can also be linked to poststructuralism, but they were more prominent in wrestling with the issue of postmodernism.) Each of these thinkers had a personal contribution to make, and in some cases knew and influenced each other; yet they did not come together as a consolidated group. Although some of them wrote for the poststructuralist periodical *Tel Quel*, headed for a time by Barthes, they issued no manifestoes nor any joint statements of policy. Nevertheless, a sufficient number of their ideas meshed to create the amalgam that has been called poststructuralism. In turn, this phenomenon factors into postmodernism, an approach that is often equated with it but which is of even wider scope, a new world-view or *episteme*.

The word "poststructural" is confusing. It suggests something that is happening after structuralism — and in opposition to it. True, poststructuralism denies logical connections between signifier and signified, neatly ordered sequences whose meanings can be predicted by a rational "subject." Like structuralism, it is largely a linguistic product, texts talking to themselves, not dealing with the outside world of human personalities and social issues. And poststructuralism, like the movement that preceded it, subordinates the individual to the prevailing language or discourse, making him an effect of a text, not its creator.

To further complicate matters, poststructuralism does not merely oppose structuralism — or part of it, as I've just said. Under the influence of Martin Heidegger and Friedrich Nietzsche, the proponents of poststructuralism try to undermine or challenge a whole panorama of values in Western civilization. This attack, it should be added parenthetically, was not direct or grounded in the everyday world; it was carried out in the realm of linguistic structures and thought patterns, including the construction of discourses, which are meant to reshape our view of reality. Targets included the capitalist economic system; members of the bourgeoisie who promote and benefit by that system and who in turn repress others; ideologies, whether capitalist or Marxist; the idea of history having a grand purpose and the accompanying belief in progress; "man" as an active individual subject, cherished by humanism, existentialism, and phenomenology; and the subject as author, with a creative intent. Further, poststructuralists oppose reasoned, logical language that supports a bourgeois capitalist society; the elevation of one term (the first) in a binary pair above another (male/female, order/chaos, for example) and all that implies in the world of gender, class, and cultures; anything centered or viewed as a universal whole ("holism" or "totality"). Everything in the foregoing list is representative of the "modern," that is, the modern era that began with the eighteenth-century Enlightenment and wound down in the late 1960s. The poststructural opponents of these positions could easily be called postmodern, and in a sense they are; but postmodernism, as we will see, casts a wider net.

So far, I have painted a negative picture of poststructuralism. Its enemies might say that Nietzschean nihilism and doubt fit it perfectly, that it has no ethical program. However, there is a positive side to poststructuralism, even at times a constructive (as well as deconstructive) social and political agenda. Although poststructuralists denied the existence of absolute truth, grand narratives, and any form of totality, they looked for desirable alternatives — smaller local narratives, differences, pluralism, and multiple discourses.

Poststructural rhetoric, dialogue, and metaphor triumph over pseudoscientific dialectics and grammar; "events" and "practices" overshadow structure. Now, the human subject, always prone to ideologies, would be molded by discourse, with ideas and language shaping and embracing the individual. With the right discourses, the way would be laid open for "liberation" and "emancipation." Taken one step further, this approach would create a favorable climate for the emergence of marginalized peoples, classes, and genders and at the same time neutralize patterns of (bourgeois capitalist) authoritarism power.

Some critics of the French poststructuralists would say this was not enough, that their approach was too timid because it did not actively intervene, as Marx and his loyal followers did, on behalf of global social and political struggles in the real world. These poststructuralists withdrew from the realm of actual encounters after the 1968 student revolts in Paris and found a safe haven in the domain of language and discourse. It was there, supported by the academy, that they continued to fight their battles. Growing conservatism and lack of social progress from the mid-1970s through the 1980s undoubtedly intensified their intellectual response, but did not persuade them to engage in political action.

When poststructuralism was exported from France to the United States in the 1970s, it carried a political aura from its country of origin. And the method began to gain favor in universities and colleges, especially in departments of English (particularly Yale), history, and American Studies, followed by anthropology and art history. Poststructuralism also became a signal for human liberation, with scholarship and teaching under its influence becoming political to one degree or another. This facet of poststructuralism has been called discourse radicalism, and its practitioners have been termed, not flatteringly, the linguistic Left. In a sense, poststructuralism gave fresh life to the now defunct New Left movement of the 1960s. Many of the premises appear to be the same, though the means are different.

## Postmodernism

Postmodernism is hard to define because it is so closely identified with the related concepts of deconstruction and poststructuralism. Some people, in fact, run them together in their thinking; but as mentioned in our earlier discussion of poststructuralism, there are some differences. Postmodernism tends to take a more sweeping view of things, encompassing every element of society and culture. Its campaign to oppose and revise the modern is carried out on a broad front, not just in selected areas. At the same time, poststructuralism and deconstruction cannot be ignored, for they constitute major ingredients of postmodernism.

It is difficult to determine precisely when postmodernism got underway. It is safe to say, though, that in the late 1960s modernism began to invite challenges by non-modern, anti-modern, and postmodern currents. Often the hints and threads of a new cultural era are evident in the dying years of the previous one, and that is certainly the case with postmodernism. Scholars have pointed out that the traits of this movement emerge as a kind of underground within modernism several years before postmodernism came into its own.

Margaret Rose has found that the word "postmodernism" was first used in 1934, and again in 1939, 1942, 1945, 1946, and 1954, but not in the sense that we understand it today (Rose, 171-72). In 1959, the sociologist C. Wright Mills employed the term "a postmodern period" to describe a fourth epoch which he viewed as the successor to "The Modern Age" and which demonstrated the disintegration of the values of the Enlightenment. (ibid., 172). This is the first time, according to Rose, that the word "postmodern" closely anticipated its current usage.

In 1971, Ihab Hassan, a literary historian and critic, wrote in some detail about the characteristics of postmodernism in a variety of fields — aesthetic, literary, technological, and philosophical — seeing that it has a broad cultural meaning, finding it concerned with deconstructing the traditional values of modernism, and discovering in it a considerable growth in "indeterminacy" (ibid., 173). This was the first coherent and systematic explication of postmodernism. From that point forward, more and more writers articulated the idea as we know it today.

Postmodernism has been a source of incredible fascination to intellectuals, and the number of books on the subject that have appeared almost monthly over the past fifteen years is mind-boggling. There is a collective sense that this is something important and compelling, and people with analytical minds are drawn to it like the proverbial moth to the flame. Writers, artists, and architects have fashioned what are called postmodern creative products, the traits of which emerged before the movement was fully named, though it did not take long for the word to be applied to the visual phenomena in question. Criticism of literature and the other arts followed suit. Today, the concept has invaded music, history, art history, philosophy, economics, political science, sociology, anthropology, geography, urban studies, science, medicine, psychology, and so on. Exponents of each of these fields have grappled with the idea of how postmodernism can be defined for their own purposes. Yet as one reads the literature generated by the various disciplines and observes recent productions in the arts, a set of common traits comes to the fore. Indeed, it could be argued that postmodernism constitutes a new epoch, a new *episteme,* something more than the usual shift of attitude from one generation to the next.

To define postmodernism, we must look at every possible angle. Although French poststructural theorists like Lyotard and Baudrillard have tried to describe the phenomenon and while their poststructural colleagues Derrida, Lacan, Barthes, and Foucault (the last two in their later phases) contribute to postmodernist thought, its traits can just as easily be observed in the arts, both fine and popular. I will follow this twofold track in the following paragraphs.

Postmodernism, like poststructuralism, is critical of modernism.

There was a feeling among the postmodernists that the values of Western civilization and its supporting apparatus and philosophy led to negative results. Most guilty, in this context, was the capitalist system. Many postmodernists saw in capitalism and its supporting mechanisms the source of war, poverty, oppression of the "Other," and a host of other transgressions. It was the self-appointed chore of those opposed to capitalism to find ways to attack and discredit it, somehow trying to remove or diminish its power. Some postmodernists, as mentioned before, did not necessarily have an alternative program, as Pauline Marie Rosenau points out (Rosenau, 143-44) but rather merely denigrated Western capitalism and let the fragments fall where they may. The fact that these postmodernists were influenced by Friedrich Nietzsche should come as no surprise, for the irrational and the negation of logic took priority in their thinking.

As it defines itself, postmodernism cannot be an approach to truth, a system, or an ideology (these things being modern). Advocates of the new approach see themselves at the opposite extreme, a kind of balancing force, the "yin" to the modernist "yang." It has been argued that postmodernism is "feminine" whereas modernism is "masculine." There is no question that modernism used the masculine paradigm to support and defend itself, a model for forward-looking aggressive scientism and the rule of logic, among many other such characteristics. Postmodernism, on the other hand, represents the reverse side of the coin, almost a polar opposite to the traits of modernism and, by implication, to the characteristics of masculinity.

Postmodernism argues with the "authorial" mode. That is to say, the individual's vision and emotions as a means of interpreting the world or his own inner space are no longer important. The celebration of the individual author under modernism smacks of elitism and privilege. Under postmodernism, a populist spirit takes over, and egalitarianism and pluralism become key concepts. There seem to be no universal laws or values. Values and codes are relative in what the architectural historian Charles Jencks has called a "situational position" in which no code is "inherently better than any other" (quoted in Rose, 160). Thus, to use Jencks' Yeats-inspired words, "Things fall together, and there is no centre, but connections" (Jencks, 350).

The multivalent content found in postmodernist creative products offers a wide variety of references and associations. These are often from the past, which is now no longer taboo but may be mined in a nostalgic fashion, quoted in accordance with the needs of the artist, architect, writer, or composer. This new nostalgic attitude is one of the principal traits of postmodernism, one that separates it sharply from modernism, which saw itself moving forward in Hegelian evolutionary steps toward ever higher goals and purposes. For the modernist the past was only a stepping-stone, one upon which each artist or creator built, without turning back. In the postmodernist use of the past, dead styles can be recycled in an eclectic fashion, combining various periods almost indiscriminately, something that is seen in paintings and sculptures as well as in architecture. Often these borrowings will be from the recent past, as close in time as the 1930s, '40s, '50s, '60s, or even the '70s and '80s. Indeed, high modernism can be the subject of quotation or imitation by the postmodernist artist, architect, or designer. But it should not be thought that this is in any way a true revival of the values of modernism: instead, it is something seen through postmodern eyes, a citation, even at times a parody.

Mention of parody leads to another dimension of postmodernism. The attitude toward the present and future need not be one of serious or prophetic illumination, as was so often the case under modernism. The idea of having a transcendent goal is dead, and in its place we can make fun of ourselves or itself, or can indulge in self-conscious bad taste—schlock or kitsch. All this clearly comes under the heading of anti-elitism.

To further accentuate the difference between the postmodernist and the modernist, one need only look at the postmodern elevation of the popular arts, the breaking down of barriers between high and low that had prevailed under modernism. Not only is popular culture accepted and recycled, but also the crassest kinds of cartoons and commercial art, including television and other examples of mass-media production, find favor. Much of this kind of thing is banal in subject matter, style, and execution, but this does not trouble the postmodernist; indeed, often this language is embraced.

As to the artistic vocabulary practiced by postmodernists, there is no single definable style. Much of the art of postmodernism is anti-form, disjunctive, fragmentary, and open. Stylistic choices seem to be infinite, following Lyotard's eclectic principle of "anything goes" (Lyotard, 76). There is a sense that innovation is no longer possible, and hence dead styles from the past are particularly appealing. Certainly, there are no more universal laws or values in the world of art, and, if there is any harmony, it could be described, in the words of Jencks, as "disharmonious harmony" (Jencks, 330). If the most experimental modern art seemed disjointed and incomprehensible, that produced by the most adventurous postmodernists is utterly anarchist, marking the end of any evidence of Enlightenment values.

There is no sense in postmodernism that anyone has a corner on truth or wishes to represent any cosmic, metaphysical concept. Like so many other elements in this world view, truth is indeterminate. The artist makes no effort to order and shape the world by making works of art; just the reverse seems to be happening: the world molds him. That world is often not the one of nature that we perceive on a daily basis, translated sympathetically, but rather a universe of media images, including photography and advertising, that sets the artist off from the intimate experience of nature. Secondhand experiences, viewed as the "precession of simulacra" (Baudrillard, 2), to use Jean Baudrillard's

expression, become central. The artist is then enmeshed in the manu-
factured illusions of mass commodity culture, and profound human
emotions seem to be irrelevant.

The artist may make clever jokes about his situation, his own role as
an artist, or the joys and tensions of living in the postmodern world.
The result can be playful and witty, enjoying a friendly relation to comic
strips and cartoons, but at times it can be depressingly detached from
any such buoyant emotions. The signifier may or may not have any relation to the signified, and, like the deconstructive critical theory that runs
parallel to and within postmodernism, it is impossible to seek an explanation for a given text. A deconstructionist will throw up his hands and
say one cannot be found.

Finally, in postmodernism, viewed very broadly, there is a breakdown of boundaries of all kinds. Whereas under late modernism the
characteristics of the separate media of painting and sculpture, for
example, were emphasized, under postmodernism the media fuse, with
painting and sculpture merging and even the traditional arts blending
with various kinds of performance art, including popular music and
rock (indeed, the intermedia quality of rock typifies the postmodern
attitude).  I have already mentioned the breakdown of the boundaries
between high or fine art and the popular arts, and those distinctions
now seem to be definitively erased.  There is, as well, a merging of male
and female, with androgynous types being favored (Boy George and
Michael Jackson, for example). An effort is made to elevate and respect
minorities, women, persons of color, and so on, offering equality and
focused attention to all who are marginalized.  By the same token, geo-
graphical boundaries have been broken down, as Marshall McLuhan had
predicted, to form a Global Village, thanks to the advent of the electronic media.  Global communication and networking makes this possible, especially through television, satellites, the Internet, and fax
machines.  The world becomes multinational.

Postmodernism is different enough in its tenets to represent a decisive break from modernism. There seems to be no facet of the older world view that was not opposed, challenged, or revised. Thus, postmodernism may be seen as a revolutionary cleansing force, a new *episteme*. A narrow definition might hold that it encompasses only linguistic structures, while others could argue that it is principally an aesthetic phenomenon, a matter of style and taste. But postmodernism is larger than this: a sweeping world view that covers a wide though varied territory. It seems that it is here to stay.

# CHAPTER 5

# ALTERNATIVE VIEWS

## Mikhail Bakhtin

Among those who rejected the Russian Formalists was the enigmatic scholar, theorist, and philosopher of language, Mikhail Bakhtin (1895-1975). A Russian, he lived most of his life in obscurity, first as an internal exile, then as a little-known teacher in Saransk, east of Moscow. He wrote prolifically on literature and literary theory, but it was difficult for him to get his non-Marxist views published during the Stalin period. However, starting in the 1950s, he gradually gained recognition among an ever-growing circle of admirers, especially after the freeing up of the intellectual climate in the Soviet Union after Stalin's death. Today, he has become something of a cult figure, winning the praise of literary scholars, linguists, and social theorists.

Perplexing is Bakhtin's relation to Marxism. Some claim, on the basis of literary treatises by Marxists V. N. Voloshinov and P. N. Medvedev, which Bakhtin is supposed to have ghost-written, that he must have shared their views. However, it is now generally believed that he did not author these texts (though he may have been influenced by their writers) and that, evidenced by the tone of his own texts, he had distanced himself from conventional Marxist ideology. This is not the only mode of thinking he rejected. He cared little for formalism and structural linguistics, especially as applied to poetry, nor did he admire the theories of Freud. What Bakhtin did like, most of all, was the medium of prose which he mined for an abundance of literary, linguistic, and social procedures. For Bakhtin, prose (the "prosaic"), much more than poetry, enabled irregularities and openness of human interaction to flourish. He popularized the term "dialogue" to suggest that the truth in any situation emerges only when two individual personalities (or characters in a novel) interact verbally. Bakhtin preferred novelistic multiple voices that were thus brought into play, acting and reacting on one another in a free, even disorderly manner, in contrast to the more formalized structured world of poetry or the traditional "monologic" novel. Related to this notion is Bakhtin's idea of "polyphony," in which the author, using Dostoyevsky as his model, invents characters (heroes) who take on a life of their own and whose diverse voices actively engage the writer. In this view, nothing human is seen as final or definitely settled.

Although Roman Jakobson admired Bakhtin, the latter held a different set of beliefs. Bakhtin opposed abstract theories, or what he called "theorism." He thought, instead, that language reflected the concrete experiences of its user, whether of his class, profession, or the like. Moreover, there are many linguistic traditions or threads that coexist in any culture (Bakhtin called this "heteroglossia"), and such language has imprinted upon it the values that accrue after many years of social usage. There are, Bakhtin believed, all kinds of "messy" irregularities in human utterance, infinite possibilities of dialogue. Ultimately, however, the author is always present, though compelled to work with the socially conditioned language he inherits.

In his later years, Bakhtin developed an extreme idea of "carnival" that extends and exaggerates some of the linguistic and social concepts just discussed. The word "carnival" suggests the irrational, a playful opposition to official, controlling norms of society. Looking at the late Middle Ages and the early Renaissance, Bakhtin celebrated folk traditions manifested in festivals, fairs, and popular pageants — of laughter, parody, and the grotesque — all things that grate against high culture. The carnivalesque encourages heteroglossia and often an irrational and conflicting multiplicity of voices, as it stresses the activity of the body and the senses. Events such as street theater not only celebrate the body but also try to break down social and class barriers, allowing the actor and observer to interact.

In most of his work, Bakhtin straddles a middle ground between the irrational and the rational, between the author's freedom and his being determined by social factors, especially as embedded in language. His distrust of totalizing theories, his belief in the "unfinalizability" of language make him an ancestor of poststructuralists like Foucault and Derrida. Like these two thinkers in their later efforts, Bakhtin distrusted semiotic structuralism, opting instead for a more varied approach to the multiplicity of utterances. His later notion of the carnivalesque foreshadows the postmodern fusion of "high" and "low" and the merging of classes just mentioned. On the other hand, Bakhtin parts company with those who later fell under his influence because he believes that past epochs or cultures must be seen in their own terms, without the distorting bias of the present. This last position endeared him to recent and current practitioners of Cultural Studies, thanks especially to his emphasis on sociocultural matters that reach beyond the aesthetic or the semiotic.

## Jürgen Habermas

Not every intellectual in the Western World was swept away by the postmodernist flood tide. There remained one vocal and convincing champion of modernism, the distinguished German philosopher and social theorist, Jürgen Habermas (b. 1929). A young second-generation Marxist affiliated with the Frankfurt School (and more politically engaged than the older members), he tried to stem the tide of postmodernism, even debating Lyotard, one of its champions, on the subject. Habermas believed the project of modernism was not yet completed and that it was a mistake to dismantle it prematurely. It might seem that Habermas tried to turn back the clock, but, strangely, he has enjoyed a solid following. This is probably because he carefully rethought the body of theory available to him after World War II and came up with new formulations and fresh ideas — though not everyone would agree with him.

Habermas, like so many other members of the Frankfurt School, believed in Hegelian Marxism, not the orthodox variety; and for a time he fell under the spell of Horkheimer, Adorno, and Marcuse. But Habermas turned away from the Frankfurt thinkers in two important ways: he did not share the pessimism many of them felt, and he did not attack the notion of totality. Instead, Habermas took a fresh look at Critical Theory (the Frankfurt variety) and under the influence of Lukács tried to reestablish its fundamental principles, in effect reinventing Hegelian Marxism in an upbeat, positive fashion. His holistic beliefs can be traced directly to the heritage of Hegel.

More than his older colleagues in the Frankfurt School, Habermas stressed the role of reason. The original group had distrusted instrumental reason — reason used for practical purposes, usually for capitalistic goals, involving domination of man and nature. And while Habermas shared this concern, he countered not with pessimism but with a theory of "communicative action." By this linguistic means, emancipation and truth would be reached through a rational, open dialogue between persons (intersubjective dialogue).

Everyday spoken exchanges, Habermas thought, would epitomize freedom and flourish without institutional domination and hegemonic control. This process would lead to truly democratic thinking, for it depended on the rational linguistic interaction of "subjects" (that is, individuals), who would raise meaningful political and ethical issues. For Habermas, "communicative action" could extend to public issues and opinion and serve as a bulwark against an alien type of rationality, the purposive or instrumental kind associated with capitalism.

Going against the intellectual fashions of the 1970s and 1980s, Habermas celebrated modernism, especially as expressed philosophically by Hegel and politically by the early Marx under Hegel's influence. Like these two figures, Habermas cherished totality in thought and social systems, anathema to the poststructuralists who deconstructed norms of this kind. Habermas valued reason, values, and morality, whereas the other side sought the irrational and issues that could not be resolved. Too, poststructural theory remained mired in matters of language, with few overt ties with the social world outside of "texts." And, as mentioned earlier, Habermas fought with Lyotard, standard bearer of postmodernism, because the Frenchman's views were so adamantly antimodern.

Habermas was, and is, an intellectual force in Germany and in the Western world generally. Although he was not heavily involved in literary criticism or history, he nonetheless influenced discourse in these and other fields, especially social thought. His worth lies not only in what he said in its own right but also in how his opposition to postmodernism revealed more fully the character — and weaknesses — of that mode of thinking.

## Louis Althusser

Like Habermas, Louis Althusser (1918-1990) was a Marxist and a philosopher with wide-ranging interests; but the latter was French, and his beliefs were very different from those of Habermas. Althusser is appropriately linked with the scientific side of Marx, the author of *Capital,* rather than the Hegelian or humanistic Marx. Althusser has been called a structuralist Marxist. Although this (as he himself said) is a misnomer, analogies to structuralism can still be drawn, for within Marx's own insistence on a rationalized "theory," elements of a structuralist mentality are found. Althusser, furthermore, took his place at the far Left of the political spectrum, being a hard-line member of the Communist party, a Leninist-Marxist and for a time a defender of Stalin. Having little use for the Frankfurt School or Western Marxism in general (he attacked Lukács and Gramsci), Althusser also grated against the emerging poststructuralists. In spite of these oppositions, the French philosopher gained a fairly large following, especially among those of Marxist persuasion.

Dominating Althusser's thinking is the idea of scientific rationality. Following Marx, he acknowledged the role of the economic base, though he saw that there were contradictions in the way it affected the superstructure. For Althusser, the superstructure, an autonomous entity that has a life of its own, takes precedence over the individual (the subject), in this view resembling the poststructural subordination of the subject to the cultural text. This structure also dominates people collectively, that is, as a social body, through various ideologies. Although these ideological forces may be diverse, even unconscious, they come together as a unified context that affects the way people think and may also repress dissent. By giving thoughtful analysis to noneconomic ideologies, Althusser set an example for a wide range of cultural studies, including literature, the fine and popular arts, science and systems of knowledge, and the like. Unlike Marx, he also took pains to point out that art does not have to be controlled by ideology.

Oddly, Althusser the rationalist extended a hand to Lacan the metapsychologist. This alliance might seem out of place at first, but there was a reason for it. Lacan (himself under the influence of Freud) showed Althusser how the structures within the unconscious mind could reveal hidden meanings underlying ordinary written and spoken language. Althusser used this technique to probe the unintended, contradictory, and revealing meanings in Marx's prose. Furthermore, Lacan's mirror stage offered Althusser a way of escaping the specter of bourgeois socialization, that caving into the pressures of capitalist society that Althusser felt Freud had wrongly expedited. By acknowledging that the child is socialized in the pre-Oedipal phase, Lacan offered a way out: if this critical procedure could somehow be altered or redirected, then the customary route to bourgeois orthodoxy would be shortcircuited and access to socialism would become more feasible. Whether this plan could ever bear fruit as proposed is of course open to question.

Althusser aggressively cut himself off from idealism, humanism, individualism, and even the "bourgeois" Marx — in other words, any pernicious vestiges of Western capitalism. Althusser revered the "real" Marx, the Marx of scientific, rational theories, at a time when Leftists felt that a return to fundamentals would be highly desirable. Terry Eagleton explains that Althusser seemed quite relevant to the late 1960s and early 1970s, a time marked by "Vietnam, civil rights, and student movements" as well as "the growth of the women's movement in Britain . . . anti-imperialist struggle in the north of Ireland, and some major offenses by the labour movement." All of this, Eagleton observed, "created a general political climate peculiarly conducive to theoretical debate on the left" (Eagleton, 1986, 1). Althusser's hard-line Marxist approach and engagement with a rigorous theory seemed just the thing at this moment in history.

Althusser is not much spoken of these days, but he was a potent influence in the 1970s. He served as a vital source of ideas for those involved in British film studies and helped shape the thinking of two key Marxist critics, the American Fredric Jameson and the British Eagleton. They, in turn, spread Althusserian ideas, among other views, to a wide audience through their books, articles, and teaching.

# CHAPTER 6

# CURRENT APPROACHES

## Cultural Studies

Beginning in the late 1980s and continuing to the present moment, the phenomenon known as Cultural Studies has challenged the power of poststructuralism. While "high theory" enjoyed tremendous popularity in the 1970s and the 1980s, now it is no longer dominant. The poststructuralists' concern with the internal workings of language and "texts," the denigration of the individual as mover and shaker, and the avoidance of direct involvement with the problems of society suddenly seemed insufficient. Social issues have become the new fashion among academics, with Cultural Studies serving as their standard-bearer. This challenge to the power of the poststructuralists has led to lively debate, with each side claiming the superiority of its own position. Having already looked at the poststructural faction, let us see what advocates of Cultural Studies believe.

The idea of Cultural Studies originated in Great Britain in the 1950s, though without, at first, bearing that name. English thinkers like Raymond Williams, Richard Hoggart, and E.P. Thompson analyzed the culture of the class-oriented society in their own country, focusing especially on the working classes. Their concern with class, reflecting their knowledge of Marxism, was combined with a belief that cultural products are not to be apprehended in their own right, as aesthetic exercises, but rather as merging with and reflective of societal values. What is implied by this view, as Williams especially pointed out, is that the popular arts or mass culture — film, television, clothing, advertising, music, cartoons, and so on — should receive the same scholarly attention as the more privileged fine (or high) arts. These cultural productions are not to be seen as "precious" and removed from society, but as part of it, as a vehicle for carrying social ideologies.

These ideas, in different ways, served as a foundation for the official institution of Cultural Studies. In 1964 Hoggart established the Centre (later Department) for Contemporary Cultural Studies (CCCS) at the University of Birmingham (England), and the directorship was held by Stuart Hall between 1969 and 1979. At the start, this was the only center of its kind, but others eventually cropped up in other public universities in Great Britain, and in time the movement was exported to the United States, Canada, and Australia. Despite the success of these centers as well as of the original CCCS, no one quite agrees on what Cultural Studies consists of, and some believers take a kind of perverse pleasure in saying it cannot be defined. Yet there are some areas of common agreement.

The subject of Cultural Studies is culture in its entirety, without prejudice toward one kind or another — Western or Third World, high or low, male or female, heterosexual or gay. It is in fact the model for multiculturalism, because minorities and marginalized groups receive equal attention and indeed are sought out. Culture, however, is not to be studied alone, but in relation to social realities, not something abstract, but life as it is lived. Although Cultural Studies does not rule out history, it is concerned primarily with things happening in the present.

As to methodology, there is no "theory," and Cultural Studies is not confined to one or even several approaches. Sometimes, in fact, the multitude of viewpoints in the field is astonishing. Practitioners claim to learn from anthropology, sociology, gender studies, media studies, identity politics, film studies, feminism and even — inconsistent as it might seem —semiology, poststructuralism, and postmodernism. This diverse assortment of intellectual currents has had some order imposed on it by Stuart Hall, who, in a 1980 "manifesto," separated out two streams in Cultural Studies: the culturalist and the structuralist.

The culturalist, reflecting Williams' liberal-humanist leanings, sees the individual (or "subject") being capable of willful actions and able to shape social life and events, present and past. The more semiotic view belonging to the structuralists sees the subject being at the mercy of a pre-existing structural network of ideas and values. Louis Althusser in tandem with psychoanalyst Jacques Lacan, via the British "film theory" approach, gave support to the structuralist, or semiotic, strain within Cultural Studies. Emphasis was placed on how people came under the influence of ideologies, systems of belief that ultimately reinforce the dominance of a capitalist state over individuals and groups. Some factions within Cultural Studies took it upon themselves to examine these ideological "messages," conscious or unconscious, particularly as they permeate popular artifacts and everyday visual imagery.

One of the proposed goals of Cultural Studies advocates is to change the dominant and dominating structures of capitalist society. This is not surprising because the field began with a Marxist examination of the effects of social class; then Cultural Studies broadened its scope to include all kinds of marginalized groups. The currently popular watchwords for the academic enterprise — "race, class, and gender" — can be attributed to this burgeoning field of study. Feminism, especially, emerges as an ally of Cultural Studies, being embraced by this general rubric yet independent of it and offering its own valuable examples of dealing with the "Other." Indeed, that entity (the Other) in all of its multiple shapes and forms becomes the principal domain of Cultural Studies as it is understood today.

Cultural Studies has enjoyed wide acceptance in American universities and colleges, especially broadening the study of literature. It seems as though this new field echoes and gives voice to a major cultural trend of the early and mid 1990s, a call for social awareness and commitment. While there was a persistent drive among poststructuralists in the 1970s and 1980s to undermine capitalism, they tried to do it in the rarefied realm of the "text," and the author, as an active agent, was swallowed up by the system. Cultural Studies, though evidently postmodern in its diversity and lack of metanarratives, was willing to stand up and argue its case in the real world.

## Feminism

Thanks to the movement toward women's liberation of the 1960s and 1970s, contemporary feminisms — the plural "feminisms" is appropriate because there is no single, unified feminism — have gained tremendous momentum and have enjoyed much influence on critical and historical studies. This impulse favoring women is diverse and divergent, often flourishing in combination with other intellectual currents such as socialism, liberal humanism, psychoanalysis, and poststructuralism. While practitioners of these hybrid views often disagree with one another, there seem to be several common bonds. Feminists promote the ascendancy of women and their release from a male-dominated, patriarchal society. Feminist criticism in its multiple voices stresses a long-neglected perspective on the creation and evaluation of cultural products, a stance that recovers formerly marginalized authors and artists of their own sex.

Within the feminist community, however, there are various schools of thought that are affected by both time and place. The positions taken by feminists have gone through a process of development and change since about 1970, reflecting generational shifts from one wave of scholars to the next. Moreover, the nationality of these thinkers has a bearing upon their approaches: for example, distinctive Anglo-American and French schools may be discerned. Then there are the questions of race and sexual preference: we can expect to encounter black feminism and lesbian feminism and various permutations of these positions.

In spite of this diversity, feminists today tend to divide themselves into two recognizable groups — cultural and poststructuralist. The first believes in essentialism, the idea that there is something unique and different in women, that characteristic female traits are to be cherished, even to the point of separatism. Women, according to this view, will seek power and free themselves from male hegemony. Some essentialists think that being biologically female, with all that this implies, is liberatory and should not be denied. This branch, called cultural feminism, has been placed in opposition to poststructural feminism by Linda Alcoff (cited in De Lauretis, 82). In these contrasting positions, the first comes off as weak in "theory," whereas the second appears more intellectual. Moreover, in poststructural feminism, the idea of the essential female is forced to dissolve: by definition, things like gender traits must be deconstructed. This poses a dilemma that seems impossible to resolve.

The debate seems to revolve around theory, that is, the question of how much feminists can and should give themselves over to poststructuralism. Cultural feminists, much concerned with issues of gender and identity, are seen, according to Teresa de Lauretis, as being satisfied with "a low-grade type of theoretical thinking" (De Lauretis, 84). Their prime concern is not with abstruse self-referential theories, whether semiotic, deconstructive, or whatever, but rather with the real world, the domain in which women function as individuals and social beings who seek their own identity. By contrast anti-essentialists, including women who interact with poststructuralism, possess "high-test" theoretical concerns (ibid.). They enter the (largely male) domain of poststructural theory, she says, because of its "political usefulness" and because it is an academic fad (ibid., 79). In addition, they can identify with poststructuralism because its adherents have attacked and tried to neutralize the entire male-dominated Western humanist tradition, which is seen as the root cause of the repression of women.

Besides having an interest in poststructuralism, the more theoretical, intellectualizing feminists, such as Gayatri Chakravorty Spivak, Julia Kristeva, Luce Irigaray, and Barbara Johnson, turn to linguistics, psychoanalysis, and Marxism (though Marxism is generally not hospitable to women). These disciplines are sometimes treated individually, but at other times in eclectic, interdisciplinary combinations. What often emerges is a fresh and vigorous perspective on meaning and symbolism in the arts, as well as a profound insight into society, especially where women's issues are concerned.

But it must be admitted that the relation of various feminisms, surveyed as a whole, to the world of theory is ambivalent. While feminist ideas have certainly influenced critical discourse, some feminists are not enthusiastic about theory, and there are those who reject the whole idea. Some (male) critical theorists linked under the banner of poststructuralism ignore feminism, and others keep it at arm's length. When it comes to recent books on theory, of which there are many, feminist critical approaches are often given brief treatment, or none at all. Yet it must be admitted that French-based critical theory, which dominated intellectual discourse during the 1970s and 1980s, finds its grip weakening. Other, more socially-oriented currents are now moving into place. Chief among them is Cultural Studies. Many feminist scholars working today fit into this tradition, not as dependent junior partners but as equals. Some of them, of course, may not wish to envision or acknowledge such an affiliation. But here, more than in French critical theory, is where they will find their intellectual counterparts.

## Visual Culture

Within the past four or five years, the phenomenon known as Visual Culture has come into its own as a fresh approach to objects and images, a kind of "new, new art history," to borrow Marsha Meskimmon's phrase (*Art History* 20 [June 1997]:331). The rise of this novel approach suggests that there is something wrong with art history as it has been practiced, a field traditionally concerned with "transhistorical truths, timeless works of art, and unchanging critical criteria" (Bryson, Holly, and Moxey, xv). Visual Culture has already replaced the typical chronological art history survey at places like Harvard, Swarthmore, and the University of California, Santa Barbara. At Harvard the new [1994] course treats the material thematically, and "introduces students to the history of methods and debates in the field, rather than asking them to memorize names, dates, and works of art" (*Art News* 96 [Jan. 1997]:102). Books on Visual Culture, like one of that title edited by Norman Bryson, Michael Ann Holly, and Keith Moxey (1994), *Good Looking: Essays on the Virtue of Images* by Barbara Stafford (1996), and *Languages of Visuality* (1996), edited by Beate Albert, are beginning to roll from the presses. And the field is starting to make inroads in the sessions held at the annual meeting of the College Art Association. Significantly, W. J. T. Mitchell's book *Picture Theory: Essays on Verbal and Visual Representation* (1994) won the Charles Rufus Morey prize offered by that organization in 1995. Yet in spite of this recognition, Visual Culture pursued to its logical conclusion, as Anne Higonnet has pointed out, "is not a tweaking of art history." It is, rather, "a fundamental disruption" (ibid., 104). But unlike traditional art history, it has as yet no theories, no master narrative. It is a youthful, amorphous medium that is still trying to find its own identity.

In his book and in two recent articles, W. J. T. Mitchell has characterized Visual Culture as well as anyone, to date. He points out that the new field — "the study of the social construction of visual experience"

— represents a "pictorial turn" that permeates a whole variety of fields and disciplines (*Art Bulletin* 77 [Dec. 1995]:540-1). It requires, he says, "conversations among art historians, film scholars, optical technologists and theorists, phenomenologists, psychoanalysts, and anthropologists" (ibid., 540). The construction of Visual Culture is thus interdisciplinary, but he warns us that its practitioners should avoid a fashionable, glib interdisciplinarity for its own sake. Mitchell prefers the idea of "indiscipline," a code word for remaining faithful to one discipline or another but finding new areas of inquiry (like Visual Culture) at the margins of a given field. Mitchell, however, consistently tips his hat to a variety of disciplines to which Visual Culture should be responsive — "art history, literary and media studies, and cultural studies" (ibid.).

Visual Culture, unlike traditional art history, may concern itself with mass culture and the popular arts (it shares this interest with the field known as Cultural Studies, but Mitchell cautions us not to regard Visual Culture as the "visual front" of Cultural Studies). For this reason, Visual Culture finds a natural home in Film Studies programs and departments. These, more than art history, deal with issues of popular culture. Yet Visual Culture, unlike film programs, is not limited to contemporary or recent materials but can easily address itself to the remote past.

"Image" (picture) vs. "Text" (or the word) has become the central issue among advocates of what I will call the new visuality. Mitchell points out in the introduction to his prize-winning book that we live in a world filled with images (pictures) and feels that in our studies we should address them as well as following our traditional reverence for texts. The new discipline indeed offers an antidote to the concern with textuality associated with structuralism and poststructuralism in the 1970s and 1980s, when everything became a text and much critical theory was dominated by the internal dialogue between one text and another, via language. Visual Culture relies in large part on sensory experience

— particularly the eye — and that provides a welcome relief to the self-referential world of linguistic relations. Aptly, Barbara Stafford articulated this tension when she wrote in her 1996 book: "I am arguing that we need to disestablish the view of cognition as aggressively linguistic. It is narcissistic tribal compulsion to overemphasize the agency of *logos* [the word] and annihilate rival imaginaries . . . " (Stafford, 7).

Stafford is perhaps the most vehement and vocal advocate for the visual. She feels that far too much attention has been given to word-text oriented thinking and that the visual has been disparaged or ignored. The seen world, she says, is a vibrant source of information, ranking with and often surpassing the semiotic as a means of gaining knowledge about a given time and/or place. Unlike Mitchell, who hesitates to become fully interdisciplinary, Stafford embraces every imaginable field, from optics to natural history, as long as it (they) shed(s) light on the object of her inquiry. And while Mitchell advocates a balanced interchange between image and text, Stafford opts for the primacy of the visual. She thus seems more emphatically avant-garde than Mitchell in her views. Or perhaps she is more retardataire: she looks backward to late nineteenth- and early twentieth-century art history, when both the visual (often aesthetic) experience and broad cultural contexts were cherished, separately or together, by the art historical community. If Stafford is leaning toward the past, perhaps she is caught up in postmodern nostalgia. But unlike so many (linguistic) postmodernists, she does not deconstruct earlier times, but rather mines them for their affirmative, positive value.

In recent conversations with friends, I have often said that encountering Visual Culture is something like rediscovering the wheel, that round object being the discipline of art history as it was practiced before it was politicized as the New Art History some fifteen or twenty years ago. The New Art History opened up the field to a panoply of approaches — Marxism, feminist, gay and lesbian theory, postcolonialism, deconstruction, semiotics, and psychoanalysis. In different ways, these varied modes helped break down the exclusive canon of great masterpieces fabricated by white Western European males and the privileging of the fine over the popular arts. In the New Art History, art was seen at one extreme as a text, without an "author"; or at the other, as functioning politically as an instrument for social, gender, or class justice. At both poles, and anywhere in between, the visual played a small part — or none at all. Indeed, "scopic regimes" (Martin Jay) or the power of the "gaze" (Norman Bryson) were to be avoided. The advent of Visual Culture, however, changed all that. Looking, experiencing through the senses (primarily visual), and feeling are on their way back. It is no longer a crime to speak of the author as maker of the work of art or of the spectator as having human (psychological and physiological) sensations.

In spite of the recent efforts to define Visual Culture, it remains a slippery concept. Perhaps it is too new to have clear-cut boundaries. Or possibly it defines itself principally by what it is not. This is Mitchell's tone in the following remarks about Visual Culture: "It names a problematic rather than a well-defined theoretical object. Unlike feminism, gender studies, or studies in race and ethnicity, it is not a political movement, not even an academic movement like cultural studies. Visuality, unlike race or gender or class, has no innate politics. Like language, it is a medium in which politics (and identification, desire, and sociability) are conducted" (*Art Bulletin* 77 [Dec. 1995]:542). From one point of view, Visual Culture may be a postmodern entity that deconstructs what is outdated and useless. But it offers new openings to those seeking to reform art history. Once again we may turn to visual sensations and experiences, welcome the interdisciplinary, rejoice not only in high art but also in the vitality of mass or popular culture, and view culture non-politically, almost from an anthropological perspective. The multidimensional Erwin Panofsky, in recent years seen as a dinosaur of art history, now enjoys renewed popularity. Mitchell calls him "an inevitable model and starting point for any general account of what is now called 'visual culture'" (Mitchell, 16).

Visual Culture may only be a passing fad. But given the inevitability of change in art-theoretical fashions, I would estimate that Visual Culture's time has come and that both semiotic poststructuralism and socially-based approaches will begin to lose ground. As with any movement — artistic or theoretical — this change will take time; but at the moment Visual Culture has a great deal of momentum and offers fresh new fields for discovery and insight.

# CONCLUSION

The preceding texts have been designed to give the reader an overview of currently popular critical approaches to art and thought. Some of these views are different from each other, and others are mutually supportive. But whatever their positions may be, they are part of today's intellectual discourse, and they are influencing thought now and have done so over the past several decades.

Of course, intellectual and cultural positions are subject to change. New theories, like movements in art, emerge every few years, and what once seemed pertinent may appear dated and no longer in the mainstream. For example, Jacques Derrida already now appears slightly off the mark. Yet this does not mean that he is no longer relevant. Bit by bit, he is becoming an historical figure whose ideas have already influenced a great many people and who still resonates in our collective consciousness today.

In writing these essays, I have tried to deal not only with concerns of the recent and more distant past, but also with matters of current interest—the latest trends in theory and critical thought. As in art, theory builds on theory, the (slightly) older serving as a foundation for new directions. It is hoped that this book, with its comprehensive glossary, will serve as the basis for understanding critical thinking and its language for years to come. If and when it begins to go out of date, I hope to present subsequent revised editions.

# GLOSSARY

by William Innes Homer

with the assistance of
Tracy Myers and Allan Antliff
with additional entries provided by

Eugene Balk

Cristina Bishop

Alan Braddock

Diana Darrow

Linda Day

John Ferguson

Cynthia Fowler

William S. Gee

Martha N. Hagood

Beth Hinderliter

Patrick Johnson

Simon Keating

Bill Keller

Susan Lake

James Martinez

Jessica Murphy

Emily Nash

Carol Nigro

Kathleen V. Ottervik

Michele Shauf

Karen Sherry

Stephen Wagner

Cartoons by Tina Waring

*"I don't know what it all means, and I'm sure I don't want to know . . ."*

# List of Terms

Brackets =subject covered in text essays

abject

agent, agency

[aleatory]

alterity

aporia

archaeology

[aura]

[author]

[binary opposition, binary pairs]

bricolage

Camp

canon

[carnival, carnivalesque]

[code]

colonialism and postcolonialism

commodification

commodity fetishism

[critical theory]

critique

decentering

denotation and connotation

diachronic and synchronic

dialetic(al)

[dialogical]

diaspora

[différence, différance]

discourse

Écriture feminine

embedded, embeddedness

episteme

epistemology

essentialism

ethnicity, race

ethnocentricity or ethnocentrism

fetish

foreground, foregrounding

foundationalism/
    anti-foundationalism

gaze

genealogy

grammatology

gynesis

hegemony

hermeneutics

[heteroglossia]

heuristic

historicism

homology

humanism, liberal humanism

hybridity

[hyperreal]

identity politics

ideology

immanence

index, indexical

instrumental, instrumentality
intentionality
[interpellation]
interrogate, interrogative
intersubjective, intersubjectivity
intertexuality
intervention
irony
liminal, liminality
logocentrism, phonocentrism
ludic
[margin, marginality]
mediation
metalanguage
metaphor
metaphysics
metonymy/metonym
New Historicism
nominalism/nominalist
normative
ontological argument
ontology
paradigm and syntagm
[paralogy]
performativity
phallocentrism
phenomenology
polysemy
pragmatism
praxis
[presence]
problematic
project

reception theory,
    reception aesthetics
reductionism
referent
[reflectionism]
reflexive, reflexivity
reify
reinscribe
representation
resistance
rhetoric
rupture/break
self-fashioning
semiotics
[sign]
simulacra
situationist
social formation
[socialist realism]
subaltern
subject, subjectivity
subject-object relations
subject position
synecdoche
teleology
textuality
topos
transcendent
transgression
trope

# GLOSSARY

**abject:** The term abject designates both a state of being in which subjectivity collapses and those objects which cause that collapse. The abject, as described by Julia Kristeva in *Powers of Horror: An Essay on Abjection* (1980), threatens subjectivity through its status of being something excluded from a pure and clean subject, that is, all that can be separated off from the body such as excreta, breast milk, tears, menstrual blood. The abject is thus described by Kristeva as a "jettisoned object, [which] is radically excluded and draws me towards the place where meaning collapses" (Kristeva, 2). Kristeva draws on the earlier work of Georges Bataille on abjection when she finds that abjection functions across a prohibition or taboo that is easily broken. Abjection — a state forever looming — represents the inability to exclude filth. The very weakness of this exclusion/prohibition, however, is what draws Kristeva to the abject. When she writes "defilement is what is jettisoned from the symbolic system" (ibid., 65), she locates all that is feminine as that which escapes the phallogocentric culture of the symbolic. The feminine, specifically the maternal, is thus characterized as having an ultimate power to challenge a culture which defines itself through exclusion. As Kristeva writes, the "demonical potential of the feminine . . . precisely on account of its power, does not succeed in differentiating itself as other but threatens one's own and clean self, which is the underpinning of any organization constituted by exclusion and hierarchies" (ibid., 65). However, while the abject may indeed have the power of disruption, as a strategy it must necessarily stay on the side of the unspeakable, the semiotic. Many contemporary artists from Cindy Sherman who photographs herself mired in filth and body fluids to Mike Kelley who celebrates himself as a "pantshitter and proud of it," have found this power of the abject absorbing and have incorporated the abject as a strategy in their artwork. (Beth Hinderliter)

**agent, agency:** The agent is a subject or "author" who actively pursues a goal. His behavior is governed by a sense of purpose, a belief that the individual can (and should) change things and indeed become an instrument of power. Those who believe in agency think that individuals, singly or in groups, can direct the course of history. In the field of sociology, there is continuing debate (agency vs. structure) between (1) those who believe that social systems have little effect on the behavior of individual agents and (2) those who think social constraints shape and determine people's actions. Deconstructionists and poststructuralists are suspicious of the idea of agency. Foucault seeks an agentless history; Derrida and Barthes wish to withhold power from the "author"; and Althusser thoroughly discredits the idea of agency. Proponents of Cultural Studies, however, welcome the role of agency in history and culture while also believing that the agent is conditioned by social forces. (William I. Homer)

**alterity:** *The Oxford English Dictionary* defines alterity as "the state of being different; diversity, 'otherness.' " Currently the word is used to refer to the identity of minority or marginalized groups: African-Americans, Native Americans, women, gays, and the like — as authors or as topics of artistic treatment. (William I. Homer)

**aporia** (from the Greek for "impassable path;" from the Latin for "doubt, perplexity"): In the literal sense, "aporia" means a passage in speech or writing that presents difficulty or creates doubt. In the context of literary criticism, it is central to the theory of deconstruction initiated by Jacques Derrida in the late 1960s (*Writing and Difference*, 1967; trans. 1976). It is frequently used to indicate a kind of impasse or conflict: a point at which a text's built-in contradictions can no longer be resolved, or at which any text can be read as saying something quite different from what it appears to be saying. The inherent, self-contradictory elements may include what is outside the text, what is not said (*dehors de text*). Deconstructive readings track down and identify those "aporias" that undermine coherent meaning, leading to the claim that a text may have so many different or contradictory meanings that it can possess no essential meaning. (Susan Lake)

**archaeology:** "Archaeology," a methodology developed by Michel Foucault, aims to uncover the history of ideas via systems of thought. Archaeology is not a specific programmatic procedure prescribed by Foucault for others to follow, but rather a strategy he applies in his own writings to diverse fields. Archaeology departs from traditional methods of study in that it does not seek to discover transcendental truths (Platonic essences), evolutionary chains of ideas, historical influence, or causality. Instead, Foucault uses the archaeological method to reveal the autonomous, unconscious, a priori structures that determine and limit what can and cannot be said within a particular discourse and to define the relationship between different discourses within a specific time period. Archaeology does not seek to recreate or redefine historical meaning through ideas expressed in representative objects or documents, as do conventional history and science, but to examine the "space" in which various objects or discourses emerge and the configurations or "fundamental codes" which make a certain discourse possible at a particular moment in time. Rather than searching for the origin or meaning of a specific discourse, Foucault attempts to uncover the structures or framework which operate well below conscious awareness and determine the range of possibility within that discourse.

In *The Archaeology of Knowledge* (1969), Foucault explains how he had previously applied archaeology to subjects such as madness, clinical medicine, and the human sciences. In each case, he examined a separate stratum of history as a concrete and discrete entity. By studying the structures which determined the social behavior and the production of knowledge within a particular discipline, he explained the emergence of new discursive practices as breaks or "mutations" rather than as linear developments. Psychiatry, for instance, was shown to be the result of a discontinuity between two types of medicine. Shortly after *The Archaeology of Knowledge* was published, Foucault adopted the "genealogical method" which was not intended to replace archaeology, but to complement it. Utilizing the two methods together, Foucault was able to show how a grid of knowledge and power determined all discursive practice within a specific time period. (Cristina Bishop)

**bricolage** (French verb — *bricoler*): In the literal sense, "bricolage" means an improvisation or a piece of handiwork composed from readily available materials or made through the transformation of "found" materials. The term is sometimes used in connection with works of art in the same sense as the word "collage."

In relation to critical theory, "bricolage" is a term used by the structural anthropologist Claude Lévi-Strauss in two works of 1962 (*Totemism* and *The Savage Mind*) to describe the process by which non-literate cultures enable themselves to explain and cope with the world. Lévi-Strauss described this process as a " 'science of the concrete' (as opposed to our . . . science of the 'abstract')" through which such cultures organize the perceptible data of the world into improvised but carefully arranged cognitive structures. Correspondences are then established between the natural and social orders, such that they are understood to mirror each other, rendering each comprehensible. (The "improvisational" or "made-up" character of these structures accounts for the use of the term "bricolage.") An example of this process in "primitive" cultures is the invention of totems, in which the individual

## bricolage

"An example of this process in "primitive" cultures is the invention of totems, in which the individual perceives similarities between her/himself and some other species and then denominates her/himself in reference to that species."

perceives similarities between her/himself and some other species and then denominates her/himself in reference to that species (e.g., "I am a bear") (Hawkes, 50). (Tracy Myers)

**Camp:** "Camp" is a sensibility, not an art movement. It is hard to talk about because intangible issues of taste are involved. The critic Susan Sontag, in a ground breaking article, "Notes on Camp," *Partisan Review* (1964), points out that Camp sees the world in aesthetic terms, in terms of pure style. The emphasis on style, in turn, denies or minimizes content (i.e., a message or meaning, including the political dimension). Camp is not limited to the fine arts; any art form (especially the decorative arts), medium, or lifestyle can be the subject of Camp treatment or Camp perception.

Camp, Sontag observes, loves "the exaggerated, the 'off' things being what they are not" (Sontag, 518). As applied to persons especially, Camp likes the exaggerated, androgyny, mannerisms of personality, theatricality, impersonation. Camp uses the past selectively for its sentimental value and/or as a source for the "acute, esoteric, and the perverse" (ibid., 521). Doing the extraordinary in a spirit of extravagance is Camp, as long as it is "special, glamorous" (ibid., 523).

If something is bad, in style or form, it is not necessarily Camp. Some bad art is too "dogged and pretentious" to be Camp (ibid., 524). The element of the fantastic is needed. "Bad" art of the past, however, can be a candidate for Camp, especially if it is viewed in a detached fashion. As certain things move into the past, become historical, and lose "content," they become subject to Camp treatment.

Camp will not identify with "extreme states of feeling, especially tragedy" (ibid., 526). Camp likes elitist detachment, but accepts vulgarity and the mass-produced object. Oscar Wilde embraced all media, all art forms, and in this way forecast the current Camp sensibility. And he also predicted the postmodern breakdown of the boundaries between "high" and "low."

Camp is possible in a jaded, bored, affluent society. It is favored by male homosexuals, who are influential creators of a significant sensibility in our time. But not all homosexuals are interested in Camp, nor are all Camp followers homosexual. (William I. Homer)

**canon:** In Biblical literature, the term originally referred to the books in the Hebrew Bible and the New Testament which were officially recognized by the Christian Church as Holy Scripture. In its secular application, it designated works considered by experts to be the genuine product of a particular artist or author (e.g., "the Shakespeare canon"). In recent decades, however, the term has accrued a broader and more subjectively determined meaning, specifying "those authors [or artists] whose works, by a cumulative consensus of authoritative critics and scholars, as well as by their conspicuous and continued influence on later authors [or artists], have come to be widely recognized as 'major.' " The "collective cultural process" by which authors (or artists) become part of the canon is called "canon formation" (Abrams, 20).

The major critical project centering on the canon during the past two decades has been a reevaluation of the criteria which have historically constituted the grounds for inclusion in or exclusion from the canon. In the fields of both literature and art history, this reevaluation has expanded the canon to include previously ignored groups, specifically, people of color, women, and those who work outside the parameters of what is generally termed "high culture." That very effort, however, has been the subject of heated debate insofar as it can amount either to the formation of alternative canons, with the resultant continued ghettoization of the group at issue, or to the establishment of canonical parity of those groups at the expense of recognition of their uniqueness. (Tracy Myers)

**colonialism and postcolonialism:** Generally, colonialism describes the forcible domination of one nation over another, a European and later American policy that prevailed during the late nineteenth and early twentieth century. Colonialism as a strategy of power domination operated through rhetorically labeling and classifying the colonized "as a population of degenerate types on the basis of racial origin, in order to justify conquest and to establish systems of administration and instruction" *(Screen* 24, no. 6 [1983]: 23). In his 1978 book, *Orientalism,* Edward Said critiqued colonialism through an exploration of European representations of the Middle East. Although Said described his criticism as post-colonial, others make a distinction between colonial critique which "considers the set of problems provided by imperialist views of the colonies" and post-colonial critique, which "examines the products of the post-colonial societies, usually texts by authors . . . who perceive themselves in direct opposition to colonialism" (Terry Goldie in Makaryk, 462). Postcolonialism reflects a shift in interest from "the imperial self's view of the other to exploration of the other as self" (Makaryk, 463). The ways in which "colonialism is viewed as an apparatus for constituting subject positions through the field of representation" is currently under debate in postcolonial discourse (Stephen Selmon in Tiffin and Lawson, 17). (Cynthia Fowler)

**commodification:** Commodification refers to the process of exchange under the capitalist system in which everything, including labor, is given a monetary value, enabling the capitalist to buy and sell commodities in an exchange system that assumes a monetary standard of equivalence potentially applicable to everything. In his influential book *History and Class Consciousness* (1925) the Marxist philosopher Georg Lukács formulated the concept of reification out of Marx's theory of commodification, arguing that, under capitalism, relations between men take on the appearance of relations between things [commodities].

Commodification is a central concept in the Situationist idea of the "spectacle" and Jean Baudrillard's "simulacrum." (Allan Antliff)

**commodity fetishism:** A concept proposed by Karl Marx in *Capital,* his history/analysis of the social and economic dynamics of labor and the production and ownership of goods. The term "fetishism" was derived by Marx from Ludwig Feuerbach's critique of religion; according to Feuerbach, goods seem to have a life of their own when, in fact, the power and capacities of those goods are really the power and capacities of humanity which are amplified by the religious imagination and given definition in religious belief. In Marx's view, commodities (goods, the objects of production) are similarly perceived and appear to have an independent existence of their own based on the interaction of economic laws. In other words, commodity fetishism transforms individual, personal relationships into material relations; thus social relationships ultimately become relationships to and between things. This leads to an inversion of subject and object, an inversion that in Marx's analysis points to the annihilation of human subjectivity. (William S. Gee)

**critique** (noun and verb): In literature, a carefully thought-out assessment or evaluation of a literary work, usually in the form of an essay or review. In philosophy, politics, the social sciences, and ideological systems, a systematic examination of a principle, idea, or institution, the objective of which is generally to determine its limits and/or internal contradictions. An example from art history: Linda Nochlin's influential article of 1971, "Why Have There Been No Great Women Artists?" is a critique of what was until that time the standard methodology of art history, in that it questions the legitimacy of a canon formulated by and consisting almost exclusively of white males. (Tracy Myers)

## commodity fetishism

"Commodity fetishism transforms individual, personal relationships into material relations; thus social relationships ultimately become relationships to and between things."

**decentering** (and its opposite, centering): To understand decentering, a poststructural concept, one must first deal with centering, which is associated with older (modernist) systems and values. That approach holds that societies (and individual human beings) possess established, definable centers or origins. Coherence, stability, logic, and rationality characterize this world view. On the other hand, poststructuralists like Derrida, Foucault, and Lacan wish to deconstruct or destabilize the idea of centering, as they also critique artists' originality. Key words become rethinking, subverting, erasure, and discontinuity. Emphasis is placed on the boundaries, or the marginalized (which have been neglected by the centered [closed] view of civilization). (William I. Homer)

**denotation and connotation** (adjectives--denotative and connotative; verbs--denote and connote): "Denotation" is the primary or dictionary meaning of a word. "Connotation" is the potential range of secondary associations or responses elicited by the word, or one of these associations. Which of the associations is evoked depends on the context in which the word is used. Example: The word "home" denotes the physical structure in which one lives, but it connotes "privacy, intimacy, and coziness," all of which are generally considered (or expected) to be embodied in and provided by that physical structure (Abrams, 35). (Tracy Myers)

**diachronic** and **synchronic** (nouns--diachrony and synchrony): Ferdinand de Saussure distinguished between these two approaches to the study of language in his *Course in General Linguistics* (1916). Diachronic study focuses on historical change in language over time; this is the method of nineteenth-century linguistics, which examined language in terms of such things as the transformation of the use of words as a result of cultural change. In opposition to this type of study, Saussure proposed a method, which he called synchronic, that viewed

*"It's signed and dated in the lower right corner, 1872."*

# diachronic and synchronic

"Diachronic study focuses on historical change in language over time
. . . the synchronic [method] views language as a complete system
operating at a given moment."

language as "a complete system operating at a given moment" (Baldick, 55). That is, rather than examining the development of language over time, he fixed his study in a specific moment, reflecting his belief that language acquires its meaning not through our knowledge of its history, but through our own competence in it. In general usage, then, diachrony refers to the flow of something over time, whereas synchrony refers to its fixity in a particular moment. (Tracy Myers)

**dialectic(al):** In its most general sense, dialectic is a method of formal reasoning in which truth is sought through the process of debate or discussion. In relation to the European philosophical tradition, specifically as elaborated by Hegel, Marx, and Engels, dialectic is the interplay of opposed or contradictory principles. This interplay is often schematized as the unification of a thesis and its opposing antithesis into a higher synthesis. The terms "dialectic" and "dialectical" figure prominently in Leftist criticism, such as that of Terry Eagleton and contributors to the journal *New German Critique.* (Tracy Myers)

**diaspora:** This term, from the Greek "scattering," originally referred to the Jewish exile. But in Cultural Studies diaspora has taken on a broader meaning. Today the word indicates voluntary or involuntary displacement of various groups — African Americans, South Asians, and people of the Caribbean, for example. Such migrants retain memories of the culture in which they were raised, even when living in exile. The diaspora space which these people inhabit may be fraught with tensions born of their hybrid state, for it stands to reason that conflicts may occur between the "home" identity of the subject and the adopted (new) environment. Diaspora studies have recently emerged on college campuses. (William I. Homer)

**discourse:** The term carries several related meanings. In its most basic sense, discourse refers to a verbal presentation or dialogue, written or spoken, on any given subject. Linguists use the word to designate a continuous utterance that is longer than an ordinary sentence. But in current theoretical usages, it is Foucault who has given discourse its most prominent meaning.

It is helpful to state what Foucault's idea of discourse does not consist of. It is not a timeless window onto a fixed ideology or set of universal truths or an abstractly constructed methodical system (in the manner of Hegel or Marx). Institutional hierarchies have no place in the world of discourse. Foucault turns away from these matters to offer a different approach, far less predictable and structured, based on the *discursive formations* that make discourses possible. These formations are the beliefs, practices, and specialized vocabulary that come together to define what is possible--and what can be said--in any given discipline or field of enterprise. Such traits are not imposed from above but, rather, represent things that people generally agree upon. Thus, discursive formations expedite discourses, a discourse being a loosely assembled set of features that define commonly held assumptions and possibilities of a particular era or discipline within an era, past or present. For example, today the medical and legal professions each have their own discourses within which to examine and adjudicate questions or, respectively, illness and contravention of the law. Within the medical discourse, the issue of euthanasia will elicit questions about the quality of a terminally ill person's life, whereas within the legal discourse it will raise issues about the legality of terminating that person's life. While there may be a degree of regularity or consistency in a discourse, it is not a consolidated system; rather, it is diverse and pluralistic in nature, the result of a network of signifiers. There can be a multiplicity of discourses and they can act and react upon each other.

Foucault wishes to avoid absolute claims to truth. Each discourse, as he sees it, regulates the knowledge appropriate to a certain field or discipline, and that knowledge implies or evokes an accompanying measure of power. So in a sense, a discourse is an instrument of power, because whoever collectively governs the power of a discourse can decide what is "true." Discourses, though, are not ideologies, for the latter are fixed systems that clearly define truth and falsehood in their own terms.

Discourses limit the place and role of the individual. In a word, human beings and their efforts follow the rules governing what may be said within the discourse; these matters are not under the control of the author. History, in turn, may be seen as a *discursive practice*; individuals are limited by the terms of the discourse to what they can utter in any era. Although discourse constitutes a kind of language, the word "discourse" is preferred by some critics to "language" because whereas the latter is rather abstract, the former accounts for "the specific contexts and relationships involved in historically produced uses of language" (Baldick, 59). (Tracy Myers and William I. Homer)

**Écriture féminine:** In 1975, the French journal *L'Arc* published Hélène Cixous's widely influential "Le Rire de la Méduse" (The Laugh of the Medusa). Translated into English in a 1976 volume of the American feminist journal *Signs*, "Le Rire de la Méduse" attempted to bring women to writing through advocating what has been since termed *Écriture féminine* — a style of writing in which women write through their bodies, or, in Cixous's words, from their "libidinal economies." This feminine libidinal economy differentiates feminine writing from masculine phallocentric writing in that women's sexual energies are not contained in any one center, but exist in a state of multiplicity and flux which thus allows *Écriture féminine* to disrupt the seeming stability of logocentric writing, that is, writing that locates the signifier within the history of Reason. Libidinal feminist writing or *Écriture féminine* is thus impossible to define as it will always, according to Cixous, "surpass the discourse that regulates the phallocentric system" (Cixous, 313). *Écriture féminine* is not, however, restricted solely to women, but to all those who are open to a new history, who reject a "unifying regulating history that homogenizes and channels forces, herding contradictions into a single battlefield" (ibid., 313). Citing texts inscribed with femininity, Cixous mentions Jean Genêt as well as Colette and Marguerite Duras. *Écriture féminine* — shifting, open, subversive — is not intended to be just a style of writing, but a writing aimed at the *"very possibility of change,* the space that can serve as a springboard for subversive thought, the precursory movement of a transformation of social and cultural structures" (ibid., 311). (Beth Hinderliter)

**embedded, embeddedness:** To be "embedded" is to be firmly fixed in the material of the surrounding environment. It is understood in poststructuralist theory that all aspects of the self are "embedded" in specific communities, life situations, and structures of power: hence the popularity of the term in poststructuralist writing, where it is frequently employed. (Allan Antliff)

**episteme** (adjective — epistemic): Another term given currency through the work of Foucault, it refers to the method of acquiring and ordering knowledge in a particular period. The episteme functions as a sort of conceptual umbrella, uniting the discourses current in that period and "guarantee[ing] their coherence within an underlying structure of implicit assumptions about the status of knowledge" (Baldick, 72). In *The Order of Things* (1966), Foucault argued, for example, that the episteme governing the period from roughly 1650 to 1880 was one of "similarity or equivalence," i.e., that knowledge was organized according to examination of the ways in which data resembled each other (xxiv). (Tracy Myers)

**epistemology** (adjective — epistemological): Epistemology is the branch of philosophy that deals with "the origin, structure, methods and validity of knowledge" (Runes, 109). In common usage, the word epistemology suggests that absolute claims to universal, permanent truths may be made. But a more flexible approach to the term would include not only seeing the objective basis for knowledge but also discovering how we know things and finding the most appropriate way to know.

The idea that essential, unchanging knowledge may be revealed by human reason is troubling to postmodernists. While Foucault speaks of the "epistemological mutation of history" (Foucault, 11), he means the shift in the historian's practice from efforts to discover "unmoving histories"— i.e., stable foundations on which historical change is grounde — to attempts to identify "the phenomena of rupture, of discontinuity" in history (ibid., 3-4). In short, Foucault posits a transformation in the way in which knowledge is organized and structured. Thus, while the words "epistemology" or "epistemological" are still used among postmodernists, the projects they traditionally designated are no longer seen as valid. (William I. Homer and Tracy Myers)


**essentialism:** In philosophical discourse, "essence" refers, very summarily, to the determinative quality which defines a thing. Kant, for example, identified it as "the primary internal principle of all that belongs to the being of a thing" (Runes, 112). In relation to cultural inquiry, "essentialism" is a critical stance that reduces the analysis of an individual's position, or the position that individual is expected to assume, to terms of some immutable characteristics of that person, for example, traits that some might view as essentially female. Postmodernists take a skeptical view of essentialism, for they believe that such matters as gender are socially constructed. (Tracy Myers)

**ethnicity, race:** Ethnicity and race are related, but they are not the same thing. While race is traditionally defined by the physical, biological attributes of a people, ethnicity refers to a group's cultural affinities, which are learned. Ethnicity, then, refers to matters such as social customs, language, belief systems, and cultural traits, including material culture. Ethnic groups may constitute a smaller or larger part of a given race; but overlapping rather than a one-to-one matching of race and ethnicity seems to be the rule. While race is slow to change, the composition of ethnic groups may be altered as a result of shifting cultural factors. Ethnicity is thus neither fixed nor stable. (William I. Homer)

**ethnocentricity or ethnocentrism:** First used in the beginning of this century by William Graham Sumner, the term "ethnocentricity" has come to be employed extensively by anthropologists, psychologists, sociologists, and other social scientists. It is variously defined as either seeing one's own culture as the best or the norm, or as the attempt to apply the values of one's own society to another. There are also various levels of ethnocentrism, ranging from not acknowledging the differences between cultures to patriotism and sexism. Ethnocentricity is generally contrasted with *cultural relativism,* which, in its simplest terms, is defined as the view that all cultures are equal, or the belief that cultures have differences that sometimes cannot be studied objectively from the framework of the researcher's own culture. Ethnocentrism can also be seen as primarily emotional, as in the case of patriotism or sexism, where hatred of a particular group is based upon often exaggerated fears of the differences between the preferred culture and the culture that is looked down upon. (Patrick Johnson)

**fetish:** "Fetish" is a term denoting an inanimate object invested with mysterious powers or revered from an irrational standpoint. Marx's analysis of "commodity fetishism" (see above) under capitalism and

Freud's discussions of sexual fetishization continue to influence contemporary work on this subject. Whereas Freud essentialized sexual fetishism as a deviation from a heterosexual "essence," Michel Foucault argued the body is a site for the deployment of numerous sexualizing discourses that evolve over time. Foucault established fetishization as a social construct with a complex history that poststructuralists are only now beginning to chart. Fetishism's relationship to gender, the origins of fetishization, its role in homosexual subcultures, and the semiotics of the fetish are a few of the avenues that have recently been explored. (Allan Antliff)

**foreground** (verb), **foregrounding:** A technique favored by the Russian Formalists and the Prague School which pushes certain literary devices or techniques ahead of others. This is often done to emphasize (or "foreground") some aspect of the language itself, at the expense of narration or representation. In poetry, especially, foregrounding stresses how something is said, especially by means of literary metaphor, rather than what is said. (William I. Homer)

**foundationalism/anti-foundationalism:** Foundationalism is associated with modernism. Exponents of this view "produce cultural things that have meaning intrinsically within themselves and so cannot be made unintelligible by what happens outside them, things that are valuable in themselves. . . (Neville, 171). The assumption of a foundational basis for elaborating philosophical systems has been a feature of Western philosophy since Plato; however, recent anti-foundational critical theory has attacked it. Deconstructionists (e.g., Derrida) search out and expose the foundations presupposed to be self-evident in a given argument. Contemporary philosophical pragmatists (e.g., Richard Rorty) argue that the search for a foundational theory of knowledge should be discarded in recognition of the inescapable relativism of all forms of knowledge. Postmodernists (e.g., Lyotard) are markedly hostile toward the notion of any single foundational truth, which they argue may come to serve authoritarian social ends. (Allan Antliff)

**gaze:** The gaze presupposes that in the act of observing the subject assumes a privileged position of knowledge vis-à-vis the object being observed. John Berger was the first to highlight the gaze in *Ways of Seeing* (1972), where he speculated that the Renaissance invention of perspective marked the rise of a new type of vision in which the all-knowing gaze of the humanist was regarded as the equivalent to God's. In the early 1970s, Foucault addressed the emergence of a "disciplinary" gaze in modern carceral institutions (*Discipline and Punish* [1979]). With the development of feminist theories in the 1970s and 80s, considerable work has gone into the engendering of the gaze as a distinctly male mode of vision. The classic statement of this thesis is Laura Mulvey's essay, "Visual Pleasure and Narrative Cinema" (*Screen* 16 [Autumn 1975]: 6-18). Mulvey drew on Freud's and Lacan's accounts of vision's role in ego development to argue that the gaze creates a sexual imbalance between the male/active/subject and the female/passive/object. Subsequently, feminist theorists, most notably Jacqueline Rose (*Sexuality in the Field of Vision* [1986]), have revised Mulvey's thesis to take into account poststructuralist critiques of the subject, situationist theory, and other issues. In the 1980s numerous and often conflicting theories of the "gaze" have been mounted by cultural historians. Martin Jay's book *Downcast Eyes* (1994) on vision and theory in twentieth-century France provides a helpful overview. (Allan Antliff)

**genealogy:** Following and referring to Friedrich Nietzsche, Michel Foucault espoused the view that traditional history consists of little more than a metaphysics of origins, wherein the intricate, accidental, and ultimately irreconcilable events of the past are reduced to convenient myths, assumptions, and truths. In place of this reductive metaphysics, Foucault proposed the practice of "genealogy" or what Nietzsche called *wirkliche Historie* (effective history), a more rigorous form of inquiry attentive to the banalities, divergences, and conflicts of past events.

The genealogist thus changes the focus of historical inquiry from supposedly originary forces — the great leaders, major movements, highest achievements, which merely enact and perpetuate history's myths — to objects closer at hand ("the body, the nervous system, nutrition, digestion, and energies . . . ," says Foucault in "Nietzsche, Genealogy, History," in *Language, Counter-Memory, Practice,* Donald F. Bouchard, ed. [Ithaca: Cornell University Press, 1977], 155.) These contain information and traces of the irreducible struggles and forces that are the real machinery of power and time. Furthermore, the genealogist demonstrates a clearer historical sense by announcing at the outset his own prejudices and position in time. Undermining the conventional tools of history, identified by Foucault as heroic realism, continuity, identity, and truth, the genealogist employs parody, dissociation, and the critique of knowledge. The powerful impact of Foucault's genealogical view is evident especially in the recent and growing literature on the history of the body and its representation, as well as in the history of science, medicine, and technology. (Alan Braddock)

**grammatology** (from the Greek grammato- [letter] and -logy [study of]: Derrida in his 1966 paper "Structure, Sign, and Play in the Discourse of the Human Sciences" and in his book *De la grammatologie* (1967) appropriates a word used in the twentieth century to describe studies of the origin and history of writing (e.g., I. J. Gelb, *Hittite Hieroglyphs* [Chicago: University of Chicago Press, 1931]) in order to indicate a theory for the act of writing upon which rests Derrida's critique of Western metaphysics.

At the heart of Derrida's grammatology is his understanding of the relationship between writing and speech and the capacity of these modes to represent thought. Derrida views the Western tradition as logocentric: a centered system based upon the notion of presence and valuing the purity of the spoken word. Derrida, however, attacks the hierarchy that places speech over writing and opts for the latter. Grammatology, therefore, is Derrida's study of writing, based on the "difference" or dissemination of meanings exerted by the play of words.

If grammatology provided a foundation for deconstruction, the term was also, by the mid-1980s, used by theorists in taking a deconstructive perspective of the cultural landscape beyond the field of literature. For example, Gregory L. Ulmer's *Applied Grammatology* (Baltimore: Johns Hopkins University Press, 1985) proposes the replacement of "deconstruction" with a "grammatology" applied to Cultural Studies, a critique that exceeds the reach of deconstruction in its (grammatology's) capacity to address performance, theater, interdisciplinary content, and electronic media. As a pedagogy, Ulmer's grammatology brings the author's subject into the "scene of teaching," writing on the curriculum the author's signature, thereby decentering disciplinary identities.

The term as defined by Derrida is embraced by postmodernists. In contrast, Ulmer's attempt to replace deconstruction with grammatology has had no lasting effect in postmodern literature. (Bill Keller)

**gynesis** (from the Greek *gyne,* meaning woman, and the suffix, *-esis,* meaning action or process): A term coined by Alice Jardine in 1985 and discussed in her book *Gynesis: Configurations of Woman and Modernity* of the same year, gynesis refers to the metaphorizing of woman, the result of postmodern questioning/rethinking of concepts such as truth and beauty as well as master narratives such as religion and philosophy. This interrogation "has brought about, within the master narratives in the West, a vast self-exploration, a questioning and turning back upon their own discourse, in an attempt to create a new *space* or *spacing within themselves* for survivals (of different kinds) . . . . This other-than-themselves is almost always a 'space' of some kind (over which the narrative has lost control), and this space has been coded as *feminine*, as *woman*" (Jardine, 25). For example, the examination of binary oppositions produces an "other" that was typically designated as "woman" or feminine: male/female, soul/body.

In this process, the exclusion and marginalization of the "other" has been reexamined and master narratives have been deconstructed. Thus, many feminists regard gynesis as a tool, offering "powerful insights for feminists since it proves alternative ways of understanding the systems of knowledge and representation that have oppressed and may continue to imprison female subjectivity" (Harris, 549). Yet, many feminists argue that "this new presentation of the irrepresentable" has continued to marginalize the feminine through the use of "male critical systems," artificially metaphorizing women and creating "nothing but the negative of the Great Western Photograph" (Jardine, 39). While Jardine views the valorization and metaphorization of woman as damaging or anti-feminist (in part, because this tends to abstract women, ignoring the real experiences of real women), she also proposes the use of gynesis as a strategy for examining "traditional systems of knowledge and repression" (Harris, 549).

Gynesis is evident in many male-authored texts, including Jean Baudrillard's investigation of seduction, Jacques Derrida's *écriture*, Michel Foucault's "madness," Jacques Lacan's *jouissance*, among others. Many feminist texts also engage in gynesis, for example, Hélène Cixous' work on writing and Julia Kristeva's exploration of linguistics. (Kathleen V. Ottervik)


**hegemony** (adjective — hegemonic): The concept of hegemony was first elaborated by the Italian Marxist Antonio Gramsci. As forumulated by Gramsci, an ideology which serves the interests of a particular class achieves hegemony when it extends "throughout all social, cultural and economic spheres of society" (Bobcock, 7). Hegemony works not by force, but by imprinting ideological values on education, law, the media, and the like. In this way the dominant group ensures that various (usually weaker) strata of society accept the status quo. The idea of hegemony is dealt with variously by the Frankfurt School, Foucault, British adherents of Cultural Studies, and Edward Said. (Allan Antliff and William I. Homer)

**hermeneutics** (adjective — hermeneutical): Hermeneutics is the theory and study of textual interpretation, "that is, a formulation of the procedures and principles involved in getting at the meaning of all written texts, including legal, expository, and literary, as well as biblical texts" (Abrams, 85). Hermeneutics originated during the seventeenth-century translation of the Bible and was used to draft the rules dictating a valid reading of the text and exegesis (or critical explanation of the scriptures). Since the nineteenth century, the term has encompassed a wider range of questions concerning philosophy and criticism. It is usually connected with the tradition of German thought beginning with Friedrich Schleiermacher and Wilhelm Dilthey and continued by Martin Heidegger and Hans-Georg Gadamer. Although the approach to hermeneutics has varied, the "question of interpretation is posed in terms of the hermeneutic circle [the problem of relating a work's parts to the work as a whole] and involves basic problems such as the possibility of establishing a determinate meaning in a text, the role of the author's intention, the historical relativity of meanings, and the status of the reader's contribution to a text's meaning" (Baldick, 97). Gadamer, for example, insists that the meaning of the text is "always co-determined" by the individual reader's experience, and therefore the possibility of one correct interpretation does not exist (ibid.). (Dianne Darrow)

**heuristic** (adjective): Aiding or leading toward discovery. A heuristic teaching method is an analytical one which encourages the student to make her/his own discoveries through the exercise of her/his own faculties. It is a means of learning or problem-solving which may utilize a trial-and-error strategy or other techniques of self-education. The solution at which one arrives through the use of such strategies is problem-specific and is not guaranteed; that is, it might be an appropriate solution for the question under study, but it will not necessarily be such for future questions of a similar nature. (Tracy Myers)

**historicism:** This term has various related meanings, but all stress the primacy of history and the historical method. Historicism flourished from about 1850, especially in Germany, until the period between the two World Wars, largely under the influence of Hegel. The following are the major tenets of historicism: everything is determined by the forces of history and thus must be studied in an historical context; the past must be seen in its own terms, with the historian submerging himself in earlier values and concepts and recreating the spirit of the time (the Zeitgeist) without the distorting lens of present-day attitudes; and history is a dynamic process with a life of its own which, while capable of being influenced by the creative action of individual agents, tends to sweep them along in its wake. Historicists see the past in terms of unfolding developments marching from epoch to epoch, each being different from, but often depending on, the one that went before. Historicists do not say that the culture-soul of a given epoch is superior to any other; the study of history suggests that all such values are relative, not absolute or unchanging.

A more recent and somewhat different view of historicism was offered by the philosopher Karl Popper in his book *The Poverty of Historicism* (1961). In this volume he describes "an approach to the social sciences which assumes that historical prediction is their principal aim, and . . . that this aim is attainable by discovering the 'rhythm' or the 'patterns,' the 'laws' or the 'trends' that underlie the evolution of history" (11). In other words, historicism posits that history is driven by a determinable and ineluctable structure of forces, so that each development is an almost inevitable product of what preceded it. An historicist analysis of the French Revolution, for example, would argue that this event was an inescapable outcome of the dissemination of the principles of the Enlightenment, because those principles encouraged the belief in the sovereignty of the "average man" which is thought to have fueled the Revolution. Historicism is also an essential element of certain Marxist critiques of history, in that those critiques assert a progression through a series of economic stages in the transition to socialism.

Historicism and periodization, which is its essential tool, have been very much in contention in recent years because of the impression they give of "a facile totalization, a seamless web of phenomena each of which, in its own way, 'expresses' some unified inner truth — a worldview or a period style or a set of structural categories which marks the whole length and breadth of the 'period' in question" (Jameson, 27). (William I. Homer and Tracy Myers)

**homology:** A concept first used in biology to point to resemblances and common traits of descent. Anthropologist Claude Lévi-Strauss applied the term to culture, especially to structural similarities in myths and languages. This idea was further articulated by the Marxist critic Lucien Goldmann in *The Hidden God* (1959), in which he asserted resemblances and relationships among class situations, world views, and artistic forms, specifically, the structure of Racine's tragedies (Baldick, 100; Jameson, 43-44). A Goldmann-type assessment of contemporary American television advertising would probably conclude that the conventionalized use in commercials of montage and rapid cutting from image to image is a homologue for (or is homologous to) the frantic, ad

hoc, transient nature of American life under late capitalism.
(Tracy Myers)

## humanism, liberal humanism: Humanism owes its origins to the

Renaissance and assumes a dominant position in the eighteenth and
nineteenth centuries (as liberal humanism). While its tenets survived into
the twentieth century, especially with existentialism and phenomenology,
postmodernists increasingly challenged and deconstructed the liberal
humanist approach to the world.

What is liberal humanism? It is not a consolidated movement or an
organized creed, but rather a set of beliefs that revolve around the primacy of the individual. With the declining faith in God's power in the
eighteenth century came an increasing stress on "man" as the originator
of all worldly ideas and perpetrator of significant deeds. In this view,
the individual is an active agent, a product of his class and environment
to some degree, but he can perfect himself by the force of his own will.

The liberal humanist relies on reason and his freedom to act; he is
no longer governed by worn out institutions, especially the Church, with
its fondness for dogma and superstition. God plays little or no role in
the thinking of the humanist. Human logic prevails as the answer to all
problems in a world characterized by "wholeness, balance, rationality,
and consistency" (Gordon E. Slethaug in Makaryk, 520). But all is not
self-centered in this scheme of things; the best of the humanists promote what they believe to be superior and imperishable moral virtues,
both in their own personal living and as a guide to society at large.
Their desire for human reform and improvement, moreover, is often
exported, via colonialism, to less powerful nations and cultures.
Although the original intent may have been to solve the "problems" of
colonized peoples, it can lead to imperialistic and unjust repression.

Liberal humanists, their postmodern critics claim, are one-sided in
their identity and in their approach to the world: they are Eurocentric,

male, heterosexual, individualistic, and rational. Their opponents point out that they are the perfect tools of bourgeois capitalism and are instrumental in perpetuating its evils. (William I. Homer)

**hybridity:** "Hybridity," a term popularized by Homi Bhabha, especially in *The Location of Culture* (1994), has become an important concept in postcolonial criticism. A hybrid identity is one that has come into contact with a multiplicity of cultures and is thus fractured, split, and unable to identify with a single culture or set of beliefs. The hybrid subject who is ambivalent towards his splitting — a splitting which contains both poles of dualistic binaries such as master/slave, colonizer/colonized, self/other set up in earlier colonial criticism such as that of Edward Said's *Orientalism* (1978) — thus offers the political possibility for change. For many postcolonial critics the problem with identity politics is its acceptance of categories. Dualistic binaries are here no longer conceived of as exterior, pitted one against the other, but are reproduced inside each person. Hybridity is thus thought to be subversive through its pulling apart of categories and its refusal to privilege either colonial authority or native submission. Hybridity, then, can account for some amount of resistance (which was occluded in Said's *Orientalism*) on the part of colonized peoples. Colonial domination is not just an imposition of the colonizers on the colonized, but is also an exchange which reinscribes Western discourse as profoundly different, changed — hybrid. Examples of hybridity in art could be that of Wilfredo Lam, the Cuban painter who synthesized a Western cubist style with Caribbean Santerian motifs or the Martinican poet Aimé Césaire who wrote in a French ruptured by an Afro-Caribbean dialect. (Beth Hinderliter)

**identity politics:** While concerns with "identity" are age-old, the term "identity politics" applies specifically to a new form of political activity which emerged in the United States in the late 1960s. Identity politics is the socio-political process by which historically marginalized groups, such as blacks, women, homosexuals, and other minorities, aim to critique the hegemony of the dominant culture (white, middle-class, heterosexual males). Thus, identity politics is both a defensive and aggressive position.

The rise of identity politics came about in an era of social agitation, such as the civil rights movement and women's liberation, which effectively fragmented (or deconstructed) prevailing social theories that stressed the universalism or commonality of human experience. Identity politics is found in various forms, including affirmative action, political correctness, and multiculturalism in school and college curricula.

Identity politics shapes the rhetoric of "truth-claims," insisting that there are ways of knowing which, although different from the dominant discourse, are equally valid and valuable. Knowledge is experience-based and, thus, is fundamentally group-specific and self-constructed; that is, knowledge is determined and defined by the members of a group based on their shared realities of oppression or denigration. These privileged claims to knowledge disband the traditional power base of those who have not shared in a particular experience, because, as Sonia Kruks points out, "it is generally claimed that outsiders have no basis from which they can legitimately evaluate the group's claims about its knowledge, or those political or moral positions that it takes on the basis of that knowledge" (Kruks, *Hypateia* 10 [Spring, 1995]: 4).

The recognition of multivalent differences has led to the formation of more narrowly defined subgroups (e.g., black lesbian feminists). By valorizing differences among groups, it becomes increasingly difficult to bridge those differences to effect common actions and mutual goals. (Karen Sherry)

**ideology:** The word ideology, central to Marxist thought and criticism, has multiple meanings and implications. In general terms, an ideology is any coordinated collection of beliefs and values (political, social, and so on) held by a group or class of people. Ideologies are rarely "neutral"; they are most often used as a source of inspiration to goad believers into action or, conversely, to reinforce acceptance of the status quo. Marx and Engels distrusted the idea of ideologies for they saw them as distortions of reality, instruments that perpetrated the beliefs and power of the ruling bourgeois capitalist class. Engels, in particular, believed that ideologies distorted economic and social reality and led to an illusory "false consciousness" (the undesirable opposite of class consciousness), that is, the contented workers' failure to realize that they live in an oppressive situation in which their real problems have not been solved. From this stems the notion, still current today, that ideologies are for nonthinking people. But within Marxism, and deriving from Marx himself, is also found the belief that ideologies can be neutral, forming what Marx called the social "superstructure." For him, the superstructure (determined by the economic "base") consisted of broad assumptions and values— political, cultural, legal, and so on.

As outlined here, ideologies can be seen as negative or neutral, proletarian or bourgeois. However they are constructed, they play a major role in Marxist social thought as well as in Marxist criticism. The more doctrinaire Marxist critics will attack art that they see as representing a bourgeois ideology. Other, more open-minded critics, however, may be satisfied just to treat works as more general symptoms of economic and social conditions, without raising the issue of ideology.
(William I. Homer)

**immanence** (adjective — immanent): In philosophical usage, the state of being present or indwelling in something. For example, an immanent cause is one the effects of which are manifest exclusively within the agent of cause, rather than transcending it. In relation to cultural theory, an example of immanence is the idea of an "immanent analysis" of a text — that is, "a dismantling or deconstruction of its parts and a description of its functioning and malfunctioning" (Jameson, 23), without reference to any kind of transcendent or external structure of meaning. (Tracy Myers)

**index, indexical:** C.S. Peirce (see entry for *Semiotics*) defined three kinds of signs: icon, index, and symbol. An index or indexical sign points to, or indicates, something close by, as smoke is a symptom of fire or fever gives evidence of illness. There is, in other words, a cause-and-effect relationship between the signified and the signifier (index). Anne Whiteside-St. Leger Lucas points out that writers may use detailed descriptions of "natural things" as indexes: "They may indicate a character's wealth, taste, milieu, social success or lack of it" (in Makaryk, 563).

A slightly different usage is found in semantics. In that field, indexicals are defined as expressions whose meanings depend upon their context: "either who utters it, or when or where it is uttered, or what object is pointed out at the time of its utterance" (Blackburn, 191). Typical indexicals are I, you, it, this, that, here, then. (William I. Homer)

**instrumental, instrumentality:** The Frankfurt School theorists Theodor Adorno and Max Horkheimer coined the term "instrumental reason" to describe the dominant function of rational thought in Western capitalist societies. In the *Dialectic of Enlightenment* (1972) Adorno and Horkheimer argued that under capitalism the exercise of reason ushered in by the Enlightenment lost its emancipatory potential, becoming instead a mere instrument for furthering capitalism's exploitation and domination of the natural world and humanity as a whole. Since Adorno and Horkheimer first formulated this critique, suspicion of the Enlightenment and the philosophical, technological, and scientific forms of reason associated with it have become important components of the postmodernist critique of modernity. (Allan Antliff)

**intentionality:** The term "intentionality" was originally used by Jeremy Bentham, an English philosopher of the Utilitarian School, to distinguish intentional or willed actions from actions that are not deliberate. However, it is now mainly associated with the work of the German philosopher Edmund Husserl, who in turn adapted it from the doctrines of his teacher Franz Brentano. An empirical psychologist, Brentano gave "intentionality" as a name to the concept that all mental processes are referential and directed towards some object. Husserl took this idea and reworked it from the viewpoint of phenomenology, a method of philosophy set forth in his own teachings and writings, especially his central work, *Ideas Pertaining to a Pure Phenomenology and to a Phenomenological Philosophy* (1913). In reshaping Brentano's use of the term, Husserl transformed intentionality from a descriptive trait of psychological processes into the defining characteristic of human consciousness itself. (Jessica Murphy)

**interrogate, interrogative:** Althusser has argued that some forms of criticism establish "an internal distance" from dominant ideologies. This enables the critic to ask questions that would not necessarily arise from the ideologies themselves, in other words, to "interrogate" them (Althusser, 204). Althusser's term has been adopted by poststructuralist literary critics, who describe texts as "interrogative" when they work to prevent the reader from identifying with a hypothetical master subject or narrator who "looks on" as the novel unfolds (see Belsey, 91). (Allan Antliff)

**intersubjective, intersubjectivity:** Refers to communication between conscious minds, that is, from one human being to another. Through efficient intersubjective relations, people can reach agreement on the common traits of their experiences. This phenomenological notion suggests that genuine communication may be possible and that a consensus about various points may be attained. Hermeneutics, with its stress on the individual's experience, draws upon the principle of intersubjectivity, but postmodernists, on the other hand, believe that language (communication) is uncertain and slippery and that it cannot lead to any kind of concrete truth. (William I. Homer)

**intertextuality:** One source credits the Soviet linguistic philosopher Mikhail Bakhtin with formulating this idea and describes it as "the ready-made quality of linguistic — and, one can add, visual — signs, that a writer or image-maker finds available in the earlier texts that a culture has produced" (Bal and Bryson, 206). Other sources attribute the term to the French theorist Julia Kristeva, who discredited structuralism for its attempt to isolate the literary text from the historical and/or psychological realities within which it is produced. Kristeva characterized the text as "a dynamic 'working' of language through the desires of the speaking subject as he or she responds to the concrete socioeconomic forces of history" and asserted that it maintains relationships with other texts (Davis, 447). The two definitions are clearly related, as both posit that texts do not exist in and are not created in a vacuum. But it should be noted that the former definition specifies a quality, whereas the latter describes a process.

An example of intertextuality in the Bakhtinian sense is Edouard Manet's appropriation and transformation of Titian's *Venus of Urbino* in *Olympia*. An example of Kristeva's conceptualization of intertextuality is the relation, asserted by art historian T.J. Clark, between the content of Manet's Olympia and the social and cultural circumstances which he believes conditioned and determined its negative popular and critical reception (Clark, 79-146). (Tracy Myers)

**intervention:** An intervention denotes the act of stepping into an argument so as to affect its course or issue. The implication is that the intervener stands apart from the dispute and approaches the controversy from a position of relative autonomy, coming between the disputants in order to redirect their debate in a more positive direction and perhaps resolve it. (Allan Antliff)

**irony:** *The Oxford English Dictionary* says it well: "A figure of speech in which the intended meaning is the opposite of that expressed by the words used; usually taking the form of sarcasm or ridicule in which laudatory expressions are used to imply condemnation or contempt." Example: "That was a smart thing to do!" (meaning very foolish). Unresolvable issues (contextual irony) in literature, particularly poetry, have been dealt with by adherents of the New Criticism that flourished in the United States in the 1940's and 1950's (New Critics were also interested in paradox and "tension"). Postmodern philosopher and theorist Richard Rorty promotes an "ironist" culture "based on contingency and poetic imagination, one that convinces by narrative rhetoric rather than by strict logical argumentation" (Groden and Kreiswirth, 627). The model for Rorty is the poet, who redescribes or retells "our histories through difficult 'vocabularies,' " rather than adhering to reason, peering into "the timeless and necessary truths about the essence of humanity and reality" (ibid.). (William I. Homer)

**liminal, liminality:** The term "liminal" stems from physiology and psychology, being at the limen or threshold between one condition and another. The idea was taken up by ethnologist Arnold van Gennep (1909) to signify the rite of passage for an initiate in a "primitive" cul-

## logocentrism

"Derrida refutes the idea that language can ever be a vessel capable of carrying a sign that will represent a totally synchronous union between a thing and its name."

ture. The subject in question will share traits of what he has been and where he is going; in other words, he will be in a transitional or in-between state. Weddings and graduations are social rituals that involve liminality, an idea that has spread to literary criticism and other fields, including art history and Cultural Studies. The transition, for example, between colonial and non-colonial identities involves liminal circumstances. (See also, *hybridity.*) Liminality belongs to the family of postmodern traits. (William I. Homer)

**logocentrism/phonocentrism:** Jacques Derrida derived the concept of "logocentrism" by combining the Greek "logos" (understood literally as "word" but also connoting wisdom) with the notion of being centered — thus, a centering on the word or Word. Derrida employs the term to describe the pervasive urge in Western philosophy to identify a first principle that contains some ultimate truth or source of meaning (a "transcendental signifier"). Such a first principle is a pure essence — an absolute from which a system of thought and language can be derived.

For Derrida, the tradition of "logocentrism" is based on a false philosophical premise: it implies that absolute knowledge can exist. Derrida refutes the idea that language can ever be a vessel capable of carrying a sign that will represent a totally synchronous union between a thing and its name, that the breach between what exists and how it is represented can be joined. Moreover, he argues that not only is language not a stable source of meaning, but also that meaning itself is mutable.

"Phonocentrism," the old idea that the spoken word is a purer reflection of the relationship between thoughts and language than the written word, is historically and logically linked to the notion of a first principle or "transcendental signifier." It has been critical to Derrida's thought to show that "phonocentrism" can be subverted. Accordingly,

he deconstructs the privileged position of speech by showing that the very act of writing challenges the ideas of logic and static language upon which logocentric/phonocentric systems rely. The constant diffusion and flux ("dissemination") which occurs in writing creates an insubstantial web of meaning which challenges the precept of fixed meaning and, consequently, the previously favored status of speech.
(Carol Nigro)

**ludic:** A term that owes its origins to the noted Dutch philosopher Johan Huizenga's book, *Homo Ludens* (1938), in which play is given a newly prominent place among human activities. In recent years, as Joseph Childers and Gary Hentzi have pointed out, poststructuralists, especially Derrida, "have celebrated the disruptive or anarchic aspects of play as an antidote to the repressive or coercive qualities of language and dominant cultural institutions" (Childers and Hentzi, 229). They also go on to note that the idea of language-play undergirds Bakhtin's notion of the carnivalesque and that "some gay critics have adopted a version of the concept to describe the liberating effects of the play of gender identities within subcultural groups" (ibid., 230).
(William I. Homer)

**mediation:** The dictionary meaning of "mediation" is the act of, or an instance of, intervention or interposition between two extremes. In relation to critical theory, however, mediation is the mechanism by which homology is achieved, that is, by which identities between different structures are established. In Marxist criticism, those structures are specified as the political, the cultural, and the economic. Jameson reformulates the concept, however, to make it less specific to Marxist analysis, hence more inclusive as an analytical tool: "[T]his operation is understood as . . . the invention of a set of terms, the strategic choice of a particular code or language, such that the same terminology can be used to analyze and articulate two quite distinct types of objects or 'texts,' or two very different structural levels of reality" (Jameson, 40).

The entire practice of the social history of art (of which T. J. Clark's *The Painting of Modern Life* [1984] is exemplary) is predicated on the notion of mediation in that it employs the language and techniques of social, political, and economic history to explain and interpret visual culture. Returning to the example of Clark's analysis of Manet's *Olympia* mentioned in the entry for intertextuality, it can be said that Clark perceives the imagery of the prostitute and the reception of that imagery to be mediated by the social and moral values which determined the status of the prostitute. (Tracy Myers)

**metalanguage** (adjective — metalingual or metalinguistic): The use of language to discuss language, as through definitions or arguments about the usage or meaning of words. Literary criticism can be considered a metalanguage, because it constitutes the use of a language to examine literature. Similarly, art criticism can be understood as a metalanguage about art, because it constitutes the analysis of art through the use of a vocabulary that concerns art.

The issue that divides theorists is whether metalanguages stand apart from and above the languages they describe, or in fact merely represent specialized uses of a general language. (Tracy Myers)

**metaphor** (adjective — metaphoric): A figure of speech "in which one thing, idea, or action" is referred to by a word or expression commonly designating another thing, idea, or action, suggesting that the two share a common quality. That quality is "assumed as an imaginary identity," rather than explicitly stated through the use of an adjective expressing that identity (Baldick, 134). For example, to say that someone is a pig is a metaphor, because the identity of qualities between that person and a pig is assumed. By contrast, to say that so-and-so is *like* a pig is a simile, because the use of the term "like" distinctly specifies the identity of qualities. A metaphor may also be used as a verb (e.g., a person's intellect may "blossom") or as an adjective (e.g., a novice may be described as "green") (ibid.). (Tracy Myers)

**metaphysics:** A major branch of philosophy dealing with the nature of reality, knowledge, God, and the universe (cosmos), metaphysics readily concerns itself with questions of materialism vs. idealism (or both = dualism). It is also directed, especially with Aristotle, toward the nature of being, that is, the issue of *ontology* (see below), which may be seen as almost synonymous with metaphysics. Postmodern theorists are suspicious of metaphysics because it seeks first principles. (William I. Homer)

**metonymy/metonym** (adjective — metonymic): A figure of speech in which the name of one thing is substituted for another by virtue of some actual relation between the two things. Examples: In the statement "According to the White House, the coup is apparently failing," the White House is a metonym for the President or the Executive branch of the United States government. In the remark, "We read Barthes," "Barthes" is used metonymically to refer to the writings of Roland Barthes. In contemporary literary theory, the term "metonymy" is often used to denote the process of association by which metonyms are produced. (Tracy Myers)

**New Historicism:** Closely related to Cultural Studies (see text) in the eyes of many scholars is the approach to history called the New Historicism. This is a much younger phenomenon, tracing its origins to the early 1980s and emerging in Berkeley, California. New Historicism is not exactly a school, and there is some debate even among those associated with it as to what it really is. However, New Historicism, like

145

Cultural Studies, is opposed to the traditional idea of history, that is, old historicism in which history progressed toward ever higher goals, following grand narratives, and having a recognizable moral purpose.

Adherents see history in relation to different disciplines, such as literature, ethnography, anthropology, art history, and other fields. They are especially concerned with the ways in which culture and societies affect each other and view social and cultural events as intertwined.

The New Historicists do not see history as a grand scheme. It would be more appropriate to say they are nonlinear in their approach, looking at smaller facets or fractions of history rather than "long-range trajectories." Oftentimes, too, instead of dealing with major figures and movements, with the stress on high culture, they use popular sources such as stories, ceremonies, and the like and deal with smaller issues, that is to say, individual and local discourses. The group tried to supplement a formalist approach by dealing much more with the historical context that affected the way literature was written. Here one can recognize the influence of Michel Foucault, who taught at Berkeley. Foucault's view of history is essentially postmodern, as is that of the New Historicists. However, this group of thinkers trusts, in varying degrees, to Marxian ideas of history, society, and the individual; they believe the individual should be submerged in a greater societal text and that the author, while recognizable, is secondary to larger social forces.

The New Historicists do not want texts to be autonomous, as in the formalist conception of literature, nor on the other hand do they wish them to be seen as representative of a whole or coherent world view shared by large numbers of people. New Historicists like Stephen Greenblatt believe that history is a series of individual discourses, being diverse and sometimes contradictory. (William I. Homer)

**nominalism/nominalist:** From "nominal," meaning that which has to do with names, nouns, words, or symbols, rather than with the things to which these verbal forms are understood to refer. In philosophy, "nominalism" is the theory that abstract terms and universals have no real, objective existence, but are instead mere "vocal utterances." Only those things which are physically perceptible and have actual physical presence are considered "real" (Runes, 227). A "nominalist" is one who subscribes to this theory. (Tracy Myers)

**normative:** Behavior or thinking governed by one norm or another, norms being culturally determined expectations about how we should act or behave. Some norms are prescribed, others simply a matter of consensus. But in both cases, normative refers to an individual's or a group's willingness to follow an established, regulatory pattern. Postmodernists, as Gordon Marshall points out, show little interest in the idea of the norm because "they tend to emphasize the complexity and diversity of meanings, and the shifting and fragmented nature of individual identities. . ." (Marshall, 359). (William I. Homer)

**ontological argument:** The term for the argument which purports to prove the existence of God. This argument has two premises: first, the name "God" is understood to refer to the greatest (i.e., most profound) thing thinkable; and second, a thing that is the greatest but lacks existence is less than a thing that is the greatest and has existence. The conclusion drawn from these premises is that God must exist, because he is the greatest (Runes, 235). (Tracy Myers)

**ontology:** In philosophy, a branch of metaphysics, namely the theory and study of the nature of being and existence, ontology investigates the question of whether a property exists apart from the individuals or objects in whom or in which that property is instanced. It distinguishes between "real existence" and "appearance" and examines "the different ways in which entities belonging to various logical categories (physical objects, numbers, universals, abstractions, etc.) may be said to exist" (Flew, 255-56).

Ontology is related to *essentialism* (see above) in that the latter proposes, first, that the properties of any object under study can be divided into those which are essential and those which are not; and second, that a study which fails to address the former is effectively impotent. In order to examine the property/ies considered essential, however, it/they must obviously first be determined. Thus, a study of essentialism necessarily requires an ontological analysis, because the property under study must be believed or proven to exist in order for it to be examined. Essentialism and ontology are, therefore, two sides of the same coin.

Like epistemology, ontology carries negative connotations — but less so — for postmodern theorists. Postmodernists shy away from the essentialist elements in ontology, just mentioned, and would reject the idea that there is some fixed, unchanging core of our being. On the other hand, current views of being are fairly flexible, and thus ontology does not carry quite the negative connotations of its related term, epistemology. (Tracy Myers and William I. Homer)

**paradigm and syntagm** (adjectives — paradigmatic and syntagmatic): In general usage, a "paradigm" is a model illustrating "some quality or relation . . . in its purest form." In structuralist theory, however, it refers to the set of all "linguistic or other units" (e.g., words having the same grammatical function) which are substitutable within a given sequence or structure (e.g., a sentence), such that the substitution of one for another does not alter the order of the sequence (Baldick, 159). "Syntagmatic," by contrast, denotes the combination of linguistic units (usually words) arranged in a meaningful sequence, e.g., in a sentence.

Linguists consider language to have two axes: the "horizontal" or syntagmatic axis of combination, in which words are ordered into a recognized sequence; and the "vertical" or paradigmatic axis of selection, in which particular words are chosen to fulfill specific functions within that sequence. To reduce these concepts to an extremely simple level, one might think of the syntagmatic dimension as the assemblage of a train along railroad tracks, and the paradigmatic dimension as the selection of the cars to be so assembled. (Tracy Myers)

**performativity:** To perform an act is to draw attention to its construction and unnaturalness. For many poststructural critics who attempt to denaturalize the humanist subject, performativity has become a strategy which enables them to show how an act or deed makes a subject, not a subject who makes the act. To claim that a self performs its identity is to argue that identity is therefore never secure or stable. Thus, performativity allows a critique of essentialist constructions of subjectivity that argue that a self has a core of certain unchangeable qualities. Feminists have taken up the performative strategy to claim that gender as different and separate from sex is performed every day. The recognition of the performativity of gender enables one to deny the construction of masculinity and femininity as fixed essences. Instead, one performs what one finds will make one's self appear convincing as a being. This "appearing as being" or the performance of femininity which radically questions the category of Being, or that of Woman, has been argued by feminists like Judith Butler in her *Gender Trouble: Feminism and the Subversion of Identity* (1990). Butler, in opting for the performative nature of gender, draws on Joan Rivière's early essay "Womanliness as Masquerade" (1929), which claimed that all femininity is performed as surface, a mask. While many such as Butler have found this collapse of distinction between "genuine womanliness" and the "masquerade" to be liberatory by allowing women to construct and perform subjectivity at will, others have found this state of "appearing as being" a threatening disallowal of a concrete and hence effective feminine subjectivity. (Beth Hinderliter)

**phallocentrism:** Since the second wave of feminism, women have increasingly fought against what they have termed the phallocentrism of culture, that is, a culture which privileges masculinity and masculine character traits while marginalizing all things feminine. Phallocentrism literally designates the phallus (the Signifier according to Jacques Lacan) as the center or origin of culture. Feminists such as Simone de Beauvoir in her book *The Second Sex* (the first English translation was in 1953) have attempted to expose the naturalization of phallocentrism and to enable women to criticize this particular construction of culture and thus to argue for change. Other feminists building upon (or populariz-ing) Jacques Derrida's ideas on deconstruction have argued that the logocentrism of Western culture — the privileging of the word as truth or origin — is also a phallogocentrism: the phallus remains the ultimate guarantor of meaning. (Beth Hinderliter)

**phenomenology:** "Phenomenology involves the description of things as one experiences them" (Hammond, Howarth, and Kent, 1), a search for essences (what is invariable about a thing or object). Taking subjective, intuitive, introspective experience as the foundation for sub-sequent philosophical investigation, the phenomenologist proceeds to construct general philosophical principles. The most important phe-nomenological theorist is Edmund Husserl, for it is largely through him that phenomenology marks twentieth-century philosophy's abandon-ment of the search for transcendental truths. Among contemporary theorists (Foucault, Derrida, and Deleuze) phenomenology is generally condemned for upholding the primacy of the subject (individual) and for seeking, in experience, a conventional unifying "foundation" for its philosophy. By and large, phenomenology has little or no relevance in current critical theory. (Allan Antliff)

**polysemy:** *Webster's Third New World Dictionary* defines "polysemy" as "multiplicity of meanings." Literary theorists have not altered this definition significantly though ambiguity is often cited as an alternative term. The difference between polysemy and ambiguity is that polysemy is concerned with multiple meanings of individual words, and ambiguity, used primarily in poetry, refers to expressions. Even though polysemy technically refers to meanings of individual words, poststructuralists have "extended [the term] to larger units including entire literary works" (Baldick, 173). (Stephen Wagner)

**pragmatism:** As a contemporary professor of the humanities, Richard Rorty transforms traditional pragmatism by linking it to Nietzschean postmodernism. That unusual wedding of ideas creates a tension between the social responsibilities of the public sphere and the individual freedoms of the private sphere. It is the role of the "liberal society" to mitigate the differences between the private and the public.

Rorty bases the "liberal society" on traditional pragmatism. Pragmatism holds that the "truth" of an idea is determined by putting it to an active test. As Dagobert Runes says: "The meaning of a proposition is its logical (physical) consequences" (Runes, 261). Charles S. Peirce, William James, and John Dewey, early pragmatists, believed that a collaborative and self-correcting social inquiry could lead to a more meaningful view of reality. In the hands of Dewey, that view led to activism in the areas of social justice and responsibility. Rorty claims an affinity with Deweyan pragmatism, but he limits the traditional role of the liberal society in order to protect the freedoms of the romantic intellectual.

Rorty receives a good deal of criticism from both the political left and right. The left claims that he is not radical enough in his political stance, while the right argues that he undercuts the intellectual foundations of democracy. (Simon Keating)

**praxis** (noun): Generally, the practical application of a theoretical model. In the Marxist critique of capitalism, praxis is said to stand in a dialectical relation to theory; thus, an essential feature of praxis (as opposed to mere action) is that it is informed by theory. Praxis is viewed as permitting the elevation of the worker above the capitalist spell of numbing labor — i.e., the worker, who is assumed to be conversant with theory, is emancipated through praxis from such labor, rather than functioning as a mere factor in "the lifeless logic of mass production" (Crow, 239). The worker's active, self-determining engagement in the dialectical process culminating in his liberation is presupposed by Jürgen Habermas in his definition of praxis (in *The Philosophical Discourse of Modernity: Twelve Lectures*) as a "self-creating action." That is, through revolutionary praxis, the laborer recuperates his selfhood from the alienating processes of capitalism. In Marxist literary theory and criticism, praxis concerns the activity of writers in society, the view that literary creation in this context consists of social praxis. (Tracy Myers)

**problematic** (noun): A term used mainly in sociology and social thought, the idea of the problematic gained currency in the 1960s and 1970s with the French Marxist philosopher Louis Althusser, who wished to establish a theoretical framework or set of boundaries for posing certain questions (or problems) and excluding others. Althusser used the scientific method, with its concept of paradigms, as his model; he thought this would stimulate an open way of thinking, in contrast to ideologies that posed problems in a way that led to a ready-made solution. In a broader sense, a problematic is "something that constitutes a problem, or an area of difficulty in a particular field of study" (*Oxford English Dictionary*, 2d ed., 1989, 291). (William I. Homer)

**project** (noun): This term was initially coined by the critical theorists of the Frankfurt School to indicate the practical implications of their theory, which is intended not simply to analyze social practices, but to change them. Jürgen Habermas, for example, describes his critical theory as a contribution to the "project" of modernity (Habermas, xix). Pauline Rosenau suggests that those pursuing projects have "a strategy, a game plan, a design, a self-justifying, often hidden goal" (Rosenau, xiii). Projects are associated mainly with modernism; for postmodernists, Rosenau observed, "this is a term of criticism" (ibid.). (Allan Antliff and Tracy Myers)

**reception theory, reception aesthetics:** A variation on reader-response criticism (the belief that a text has no absolute, objective meaning, but that its interpretation depends on the interaction between the reader and the text) proposed by the German historian and critic Hans Robert Jauss (1967). Grounding his ideas in Hans Georg Gadamer's philosophical hermeneutics and Martin Heidegger's phenomenology, Jauss pointed out that each reader comes to a text with a "horizon of expectations," that is, a body of experience and knowledge about literature already in hand. Reception theory speaks not only of the individual reader (favored by reader-response theory) but also of the collective knowledge of readers who have gained literary experience over time. In this way, Jauss introduced the dimension of history to the reader's encounter with texts. Characteristic of reception theory is a living, fluctuating dialogue between historically informed readers and texts, the aesthetic integrity of which Jauss also values. By striking this balance, Jauss satisfies "the Marxist demand for historical mediation while retaining the formalist advances in the realm of aesthetic perception" (Robert C. Holub in Makaryk, 14). (William I. Homer)

### reflexivity

"Reflexivity occurs if the subject reflects on a given object and in the process alters his view and knowledge of that object."

**reductionism:** A view that artificially boils down (or reduces) complex or diverse issues into a simpler, all-encompassing explanation. In postmodern usage, this is seen as a negative procedure because it ignores differences in order to force things into some sort of overarching, basic pattern. As Gordon Marshall points out, "Some forms of Marxism, in which economic relations are supposed wholly to determine social and political life, are . . . commonly criticized as economic reductionism" (Marshall, 441). (William I. Homer)

**referent:** The thing or person to which a verbal expression refers. In C. S. Peirce's system of semotics, a sign refers to something (a referent) outside the linguistic system, that is, an entity in the real world. Saussure's semiotics, however, does not take this literal view. Instead of positing a specific, identifiable referent, Saussure prefers the term "signified" and points out that "the connection between signifier and signified is arbitrary and conventional" and that an actual referent "is unnecessary and is always absorbed in the conceptual notion of the signified" (Childers and Hentzi, 259). (William I. Homer)

**reflexive, reflexivity:** These are slippery terms. Let us begin with Webster's basic definition of "reflexive": "(a): directed or turned back on itself, (b): marked by or capable of reflection." As Scott Lash observes, "Reflexivity assumes (1) a subject, (2) an object, and (3) a medium of reflection" (Lash, 258). Reflexivity occurs if the subject reflects on a given object and in the process alters his view and knowledge of that object. In other words, this involves a kind of intellectual feed-back, the kind we have, for instance, when history is used to make history. Lash goes on to say that "reflexivity can also mean the reflection of the subject on the subject itself" (also called "self-reflexivity") (Lash, 259). The mind, in a sense, comes to better know itself and, through this knowledge, to think differently, perhaps more productively. Anthony Giddens

## reification

"Poststructuralism and other contemporary schools of critical thought have negatively valued the idea of reification because it assigns too great a dimension of reality to abstractions."

argues that reflexivity is a distinctive trait of modernism. In his words, it "refers to the susceptibility of most aspects of social activity, and material relations with nature, to chronic revision in the light of new information and knowledge" (Giddens, 20). (William I. Homer)

**reify** (noun — reification): To make the abstract concrete. Reification is a central concept in the Marxist critique of the structural characteristics of capitalist society (as distinct from, simply, the capitalist economic system). In this context, Georg Lukács used the term to describe what he considered the most basic feature of commodity capitalism — viz., "that a relation between people takes on the character of a thing and thus acquires a 'phantom objectivity,' an autonomy that seems so strictly rational and all-embracing as to conceal every trace of its fundamental nature: the relation between people" (Lukács, 83). According to Lukács, the capitalist systems of rationalization and specialization destroy humanity's connection (both physical and psychic) to the [whole] objects it produces and, with this, its sense of intimate knowledge of the physical, material world.

Poststructuralism and other contemporary schools of critical thought have negatively valued the idea of reification because it assigns too great a dimension of reality to abstractions. Additionally, such schools consider the practice of critique to stand in opposition to reification, because the latter suggests an unquestionable inscription of its findings in stone that forecloses the kind of inquiry which lies at the heart of open debate that is the necessary condition of a critique. (Tracy Myers)

**reinscribe:** In the deconstructive literary criticism of Jacques Derrida, reinscription is one of two "strategic 'moves' " employed in interpretation. The first of these "moves" is "the reversal of Western culture's important hierarchies"— e.g., male/female, nature/culture, truth/error, etc. (Davis, 410). That is, whereas in each case the first term of these dichotomies has traditionally been valued more highly than the second, Derrida reverses their hierarchy so as to confound traditional configurations of comprehension and explication. Derrida's second "move," which is designed to prevent the mere re-hierarchization of these terms, is to insert (i.e., reinscribe) "the newly inferior term within the class of the newly superior term" (ibid.). Example: Whereas in the Western world males have historically been seen as somehow superior to females, a Derridian deconstruction of the issue of gender entails (1) a reversal of this hierarchy, and (2) the reinscription of its terms such that the female (or "archi-woman") becomes the primary term, and the male is viewed as "a species or special instance of archi-woman" (ibid., 411). Thus, experience is interpreted in relation not to male authority, but to female authority. Derrida's aim in the project of deconstruction is a radical restructuring of the thought process.

An application of the concept of reinscription within the field of art history is in relation to the object/viewer hierarchy implicit in formalist criticism. Strict formalist analysis ranks the object as superior to the viewer in its concern with the perceptible, physical qualities of the work of art. By contrast, *reception theory* (see above) specifically embodies the notion that the viewer is an active participant in the construction of the art object's meaning. Reception theory thus first overturns the traditional object/viewer hierarchy and then reinscribes its second term (now, the art object) into its first by reconstituting interpretation of that object in terms of the viewer. (Tracy Myers)

**representation:**  Generally, this term refers to the depiction or representing of a person, place, time, or thing.  The theory of representation follows a modernist belief that "reality" (or truth) can accurately be mirrored by and through language.  In art and the social sciences, there is now great concern with the politics of representation. Postmodernists and poststructuralists are critical of representation, believing that it is not and cannot be neutral because it is always already a re-presentation. They challenge its authority, its claim to possess some absolute truth or epistemological value.  They work to expose the domination and subjugation inscribed within the representational systems of the Western world (see Owens, 88-91).  "Modernism's formulation of the problem of representation," Fredric Jameson writes, "[was] borrowed from a religious terminology which defines representation as a 'figuration,' a dialectic of the letter and spirit, a 'picture language' that embodies, expresses and transmits otherwise inexpressible truths" (Jameson, *October* 17 [Summer 1981]: 112).  Postmodernism, on the other hand, is characterized by its "resolution to use representation against itself to destroy the binding or absolute status of any representation."  Postmodernists and poststructuralists work to demonstrate that any depiction of reality is fiction, produced and sustained only by its cultural representation (Owens, 110-111).  (Linda Day)

**resistance:**  Resistance is a complex and enduring topic in critical theory.  Italian Marxist Antonio Gramsci argued that dominant class(es) or group(s) exercise ideological hegemony in the shaping of society's values, ideals, objectives, and cultural meanings, but that this hegemony is unstable and under constant resistance from below.  Cultural theorist Dick Hebdige developed Gramsci's insights in his analysis of youth culture, where products bearing the mark of the hegemonic values of bourgeois capitalism are appropriated and rearticulated to produce oppositional meanings (see *Subculture: The Meaning of Style* [1979]).

Foucault integrated resistance into his theory of power/knowledge, arguing that it was an inherent aspect of the all-pervasive operations of power through which identities are negotiated and structured (see *Power/Knowledge* [1980]). By way of constrast, some feminists continue to insist that resistance is inseparable from identity and that identity is founded on essential differences between the genders. Similar arguments have been raised in postcolonial studies, where theories of resistance through identity hold tremendous attraction but have also been sharply debated. (Allan Antliff)

**rhetoric:** A classical art of using language skills to persuade others. It was considered to be an essential accomplishment in classical times and was written on by many people, for example, Aristotle's *Rhetoric*, Quintilian's *Institutio oratoria*, Cicero's *De inventione, De optimo genere oratorum, De oratore.* The rules of rhetoric are divided into five parts in a logical order; invention, arrangement, style, memory, and delivery. Using all these parts will give a person the advantage in any oral debate of persuasive speech.

Rhetoric has played a large part in Western critical thinking. For Kant, it opposed free individual choice. He believed that any speech, no matter how eloquently put, moves people mechanically to believe or disbelieve important matters. In recent times, writers have tried to play down the negative side of rhetoric, trying to show its positive elements. James Aune has stated: "True rhetoric would allow human beings to escape the numbing experience of their own powerlessness without lapsing into senseless violence" (Aune, 92). (James Martinez)

**rupture/break:** A concept Michel Foucault borrowed from philosopher of science Gaston Bachelard. Foucault's *The History of Madness, The Birth of the Clinic, The Order of Things,* and *The Archaeology of Knowledge* are all concerned with epistemic breaks in which new disciplines appear and certain older ones fall into rapid decline. The rupture/break is bound up with Foucault's historical "genealogies," which dismiss the continuities of a theory of origins in favor of charting the sudden appearance, growth, and decline of diverse social practices and concepts. Louis Althusser also popularized the "epistemic break" in his discussion of Marx's development from "ideological humanist" to "scientist." Althusser argued that *Capital* represented a new scientific theory of development ("historical materialism") in which the subject was understood not morally or ideologically, but through a "knowledge-producing science" (Althusser and Balibar, 30-33). (Allan Antliff)

**self-fashioning:** Historian Stephen Greenblatt has defined the power to impose an identity upon oneself, or "self-fashioning," as a dialectic between the subject and the social structures that govern the generation of identities (see *Renaissance Self-fashioning* [1980]). In poststructuralist theory, self-fashioning does not posit the construction of an autonomous, modernist self: rather, it implies that the subject is indivisibly tied to the larger cultural patterns and histories of a given period. (Allan Antliff)

**semiotics:** The study of signs, developed in relation to logic and language but extended to encompass the visual arts as well as other disciplines. The original concept of semiotics was established simultaneously and independently by the American philosopher Charles Sanders Peirce and the Swiss linguist Ferdinand de Saussure.

Peirce, a logician, proposed his theory of semiosis as a dynamic process of signification composed of three elements. The first is the sign or "representamen," which stands for something else. The second is the "interpretant," or the mental image the recipient forms of the sign. The third is the object or "referent," which is the thing for which the sign stands. The dynamism in his theory stems from the nature of the interpretant, which is constantly shifting: no viewer forms only one association when confronted with an image, and thus each new mental image leads to a new sign in an infinitely changing process. Another triad set up by Peirce is the distinction between three categories of signs: the "icon," which has inherent similarities to the thing it signifies (e.g., a portrait to the person it depicts); the "index," which has a causal relation to the signified (e.g., a bullet hole to a shot); and the "symbol," which has only a conventionalized relation to its object (e.g., a red traffic light to the command "stop") (Abrams, 17).

Saussure's system, called "semiology," is distinct from Peirce's semiotics. The key elements in Saussure's theory of semiology are that language is a system of signs, that meaning results from the relationships between these signs, and that a sign can be broken down into components termed the "signifier" and the "signified," whose relationship is arbitrary and based only on convention. Saussure's view of signs is static and can be called "structuralist" in that it seeks an overall set of rules governing language at a fixed moment. The focus of his interest is on *langue,* which is the system of language underlying the use of signs, rather than on *parole,* which is only a particular instance of language, such as a specific utterance.

Unlike Peirce's dynamic theory of semiotics, which provides an interpretive model for art by virtue of its concern with the response of the viewer, Saussure's more static approach is less easily applicable to the study of the visual arts. Because of Saussure's emphatic basis in verbal models, it is more difficult to shift to visual ones. Two of the problems in making this transition are how to break down the visual medium into units as clear as those that make up language and how to reconcile the Saussurean claim of the arbitrariness of all signs (Bal and Bryson, 193). (Emily Nash)

**simulacra** (noun, plural of simulacrum, verb — simulation): Images operating as free-floating signs that refer only to themselves, rather than to any preexisting reality or referent, simulacra appear in late capitalist culture, according to Jean Baudrillard (Baudrillard, 1983). Baudrillard posits four "successive phases of the image": (1) images reflect reality; (2) they mask and pervert reality; (3) they mark the absence of a basic reality. In the final phase (4), images are replaced by simulacra, which have no relationship to reality at all (Baudrillard, 1988, 170). Simulation is distinguished from imitation, reduplication, and parody in that all except simulation refer to an original (ibid., 167). (Martha N. Hagood)

**situationist:** Situationist refers to those who engage in the theoretical and practical activity of constructing situations capable of radically transforming everyday life by releasing the "passional qualities" that capitalism strives to suppress. The situationists formed an International in 1957 and published twelve issues of a journal, *Internationale Situationniste,* until 1969. They played an important role in the revolutionary events of May 1968 in France but disbanded in disarray in 1972. Situationist theses and tactics continue to circulate and develop, notably in the work of Jean Baudrillard and the art historian T.J. Clark. Situationists argue that modern capitalism has commodified knowledge, culture, creativity, and imagination, turning human experience into a spectacular array of goods which the passive masses consume. The task of the situationist is to disrupt the alienating society of the spectacle and return humanity to an authentic life of pleasure, creativity, and invention. (Allan Antliff)

**social formation:** In a superficial sense, the term "social formation," favored by Marxists, is simply another word for society. But as used by Althusser, this concept has a wider and more complex meaning. For him, the social formation is a way of revising Marx's mechanistic notion of the superstructure to make it less dependent on the economic

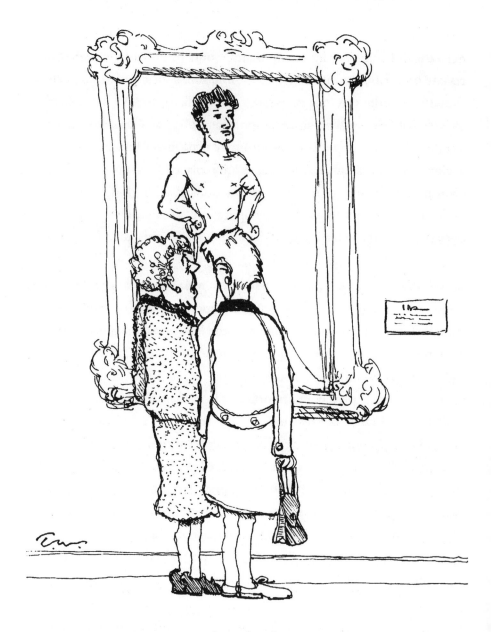

### situationist

"The task of the situationist is to disrupt the alienating society of the spectacle and return humanity to an authentic life of pleasure, creativity, and invention."

"base," of seeing various forces--economic, political, ideological, and theoretical--becoming dominant at different moments of history. This revised view of the strict Marxist base/superstructure model gives more flexibility to critics. As John Thurston points out: "Writers do not have to be judged by how realistically they reflect society, but may be seen to stand in a more complex, partly autonomous relationship to that society. . ." (Thurston in Groden and Kreiswirth, 628). (William I. Homer)

**subaltern:** Gayatri Chakravorty Spivak has problematized the subaltern (a person of inferior rank or status) in relation to poststructural theory and imperialism (Spivak in Nelson and Grossberg, eds.). Spivak argues that discussions of colonialization and post-colonialization maintain a division between "those who act and struggle" (the subaltern) and those who "act and speak" (the theorizing intellectual) (ibid., 275). The task for the poststructuralist, she suggests, is to reexamine the role of the theorist in imperialist discourses. (Allan Antliff)

**subject, subjectivity:** Exploring subjectivity has been the central preoccupation of philosophy, psychology, and other human sciences in the modern era. The notion of subjectivity, allegedly invented by liberal humanism, presupposes a unitary self (or subject) with conscious intentions and a psychological inner life. The postmodern reformulation of the "subject" — as opposed to the individual — attacks this notion of the self. The postmodernist reads the subject as fragmented or decentered, the product of multiple culturally-charged values present in language or ideology, rather than a set of singular determinations arising from subjective experience. As Hans Bertens points out: "The autonomous and stable subject of modernity has been replaced by a postmodern agent whose identity is largely other-determined and always in process . . . " (Bertens, 9). This notion is in tune with the postmodern idea of the death of the author. On the other hand, Pauline Rosenau finds that some social scientists have opted for the rebirth of "the post-modern individual" and welcome the "return of the new subject" (Rosenau, 21). (Allan Antliff and William I. Homer)

**subject-object relations:** First, a basic two-part definition is needed. The "subject" is essentially as described above, that is, a self-conscious perceiving person who looks at and acts upon things outside his own ego. These external things, whatever they may be, are called the "object." The dialectic between subject and object became particularly prominent in the teachings of Immanuel Kant, who, at the end of the eighteenth century, gave special attention to the individual's consciousness as the subjective lens through which persons and things are seen. These objects of perception, in turn, exist outside of the observer, and thus we have a dichotomy between subject and object that characterizes the modern epoch, especially its scientific method with its claims to objectivity.

Generally, postmodernists have no time for the subject-object division because they discredit the first term in this binary pair. The subject, they believe, has no particular identity but is subsumed in and becomes a product of a text or discourse. Thus, there can be no subject-object polarity if there is no effective subject. It should not come as a surprise that postmodernists have turned their backs on phenomenology and existentialism, both of which depend on subject-object relations. (William I. Homer)

**subject position:** There are those (e.g., Foucault, Kristeva, Althusser) who believe that the "subject" (the individual or author) is determined by a discursive practice, placement within a larger governing "text," or an ideology. The positioning of the subject within a governing network of external forces is called the "subject position." Drawing attention to the subject — Althusser uses the word "interpellates" — does not, however, confer on the subject the power of an independent agent. (William I. Homer)

**synecdoche:** A form of *metonymy* (see above) in which (1) the name of a part is substituted for that of the whole, or vice versa, or (2) the specific images the general, or vice versa. An example of the first case is the use of the term "brain" to denote a highly intelligent person, whose most important "part" is the mind which enables her/him to perform intellectual labor. An example of the second case is the use of the phrase "a barrel of monkeys" to denote a funny, gregarious person. (Tracy Myers)

**teleology** (from the Greek *telos,* meaning "end" or "completion"): The theory of the existence of design in nature. Teleology refers to the belief that all activity is directed toward an end and that all phenomena are shaped by a divine purpose. The term, introduced by the German philosopher/mathematician Christian Wolff (1679-1754), denotes the philosophical doctrine that seeks to understand activity through an examination of final results. Teleology "explains the past and the present in terms of the future," but does not necessarily "imply personal consciousness, volition, or intended purpose" (Runes, 331). In other words, the final outcome of an action determines the nature of that action, although the performance of that action might be purely instinctual. The teleological argument, one of the standard arguments for the existence of God, maintains that the purposive design or order which exists in the universe is proof of the existence of an intelligent designer. In teleological ethics, the rightness of a decision or action is based upon the ultimate good of its consequences.

In the context of contemporary art history and criticism, "teleology" often has a negative connotation. For example, Thomas Crow writes that those with a postmodernist bias would dismiss Clement Greenberg's model of modernism as "an arbitrary and arid teleology," that is, a progressionist or goal-oriented conception of artistic activity (Crow, 8). (Eugene Balk)

**textuality:** In poststructural literary theory, textuality stands for a new interpretation of literary texts, which requires that the roles of author and reader as the interpreters of a text be reversed. The principal exponent of this view is the critic Roland Barthes, who proclaimed the "death of the author" in an essay of the same name (in *Image-Music-Text* [1977]). Barthes sees texts as diffuse, as opposed to definite, with no fixed beginnings or endings and no hierarchy within the text to convey any sense of its levels of significance. The language of the text outweighs the author's role in writing the text; therefore, the reader is made the focus of the language of the text. With language gaining ascendancy over the author, the role of the reader must change from one of consumer to producer. Texuality stands in opposition to (modernist) subjectivity. (John Ferguson)

**topos:** A term for "a motif commonly found in literary works" (Baldick, 226). The condition of the laboring classes in nineteenth-century Paris is, for example, a topos of Emile Zola's oeuvre. In relation to contemporary visual arts, the fragmentation of postmodern life can be considered a topos expressed in video and advertising culture. A topos may also be "a conventionalized expression or passage in a text which comes to be used as a resource for the composition of other texts" (Preminger and Brogan, 1294). Topoi (the plural) can be seen as commonplaces, the result of a reversion to formulas. (Tracy Myers and William I. Homer)

**transcendent:** Most generally, that which is transcendent surpasses normal limitations. In philosophical discourse, however, the transcendent refers more particularly to that which lies beyond material existence or human experience and comprehension. The idea of transcendence has historically necessitated a bifurcation of reality into a horizontal experiential axis and a vertical transcendent axis. The horizontal plane of earthly life and the vertical plane of transcendental reality thus compose the dual nature of existence. Plato, for example, positions the Forms (the transcendent) beyond perceptual experience and the mind. Aristotelian philosophy also integrates the dual nature of reality as it posits God (the transcendent) as the "final cause" of the universe and yet altogether separate from it.

Modern critical debate on transcendence has been largely influenced by both Kant's and Wittgenstein's circumscriptions of the extent of knowledge and understanding by, respectively, the categorical structure of the mind and the nature of language. Precisely because the locus of the transcendent is by definition indeterminable, theories of aesthetics and hermeneutics which invoke the notion of transcendence and the "ineffable" are problematic. To the extent that they seek to incorporate what is beyond expression, theories which include the transcendent paradoxically seek to discuss what they admit is beyond conceptualization. (Michele Shauf)

**transgression:** To "transgress" is to break, violate, or go beyond the limits of a boundary. In the late 1960s and early 1970s Barthes, Kristeva, Derrida, Foucault, and others associated with the Parisian *Tel Quel* group theorized modernist transgressions of discursive norms in literature. The key theorist on which they drew for their ideas was the dissident Surrealist Georges Bataille. In fact, many of the key words we associate with poststructuralist work on the body, textuality, and transgression — expenditure, excess, boundary, heterogeneity, sovereignty —

were originally expounded by Bataille in his theoretical essays on sexuality. (Allan Antliff)

**trope:** From the Greek, "turn," i.e., turn of phrase, or figure of speech. In rhetoric, this involves the use of words in a manner that departs from their standard or usual meaning. There are four principal tropes: *metaphor, metonymy, synecdoche,* and *irony* (all covered above in separate entries). Structuralists use tropes to analyze not only linguistic structures but also historical and cultural patterns (examples are found in the writings of Roman Jakobson and Claude Lévi-Strauss). Poststructuralists (e.g., Derrida, J. Hillis Miller, Paul de Man) see tropes as essential in all language. For the poststructuralists, language is unstable, immutable, always changing; the presence of tropes makes it impossible to pin down exact meanings. Moreover, poststructuralists do not wish to limit a metaphorical approach to literature alone: it should be applied to every possible discourse, including the mundane and ordinary. Hayden White, an historian linked to poststructuralism, argued in favor of tropes in his treatment of nineteenth-century consciousness and history in Europe. White encourages a creative, poetic, or "tropic" view of historical writing that rejects the older, orderly, positivistic, and "objective" approach to the past. (William I. Homer)

# REFERENCES

Abrams, M.H. *A Glossary of Literary Terms.* 5th ed. Chicago: Holt, Rinehart and Winston, 1988.

Althusser, Louis, and Etienne Balibar. *Reading Capital.* London: Verso, 1970.

Aune, James. *Rhetoric and Marxism.* Boulder, CO: Westview Press, 1984.

Bal, Mieke, and Norman Bryson. "Semiotics and Art History." *Art Bulletin 73* (June 1991):174-208.

Baldick, Chris. *The Concise Oxford Dictionary of Literary Terms.* Oxford: Oxford University Press, 1990.

Barthes, Roland. *Elements of Semiology.* Trans. Annette Lavers and Colin Smith. New York: Hill and Wang, 1968.

Baudrillard, Jean. *Selected Writings.* Ed. by Mark Poster. Stanford: Stanford University Press, 1988.

———— *Simulations.* Trans. Paul Foss, Paul Patton, and Philip Beitchman. New York: Semiotext(e), 1983.

Belsey, Catharine. *Critical Practice.* London: Methuen, 1980.

Berman, Marshall. *All That is Solid Melts into Air: The Experience of Modernity.* New York: Penguin Books, 1988.

Bertens, Hans. *The Idea of the Postmodern: A History.* London and New York: Routledge, 1995.

Best, Steven, and Douglas Kellner. *Postmodern Theory: Critical Interrogations.* New York: Guilford Press, 1991.

Bhabha, Homi. *The Location of Culture.* New York: Routledge, 1994.

Bobcock, Robert. *Hegemony.* London: Tavistock Publications, 1986.

Bryson, Norman, Michael Ann Holly, and Keith Moxey, eds. *Visual Culture: Images and Interpretations.* Hanover, NH, and London: Wesleyan University Press, published by University Press of New England, 1994.

Burnham, Jack. *The Structure of Art.* New York: Braziller, 1971.

Butler, Judith. *Gender Trouble: Feminism and the Subversion of Identity.* New York: Routledge, 1990.

Childers, Joseph, and Gary Hentzi, eds. *The Columbia Dictionary of Modern Literary and Cultural Criticism.* New York: Columbia University Press, 1995.

Cixous, Hélène. "The Laugh of the Medusa." in *Critical Theory since 1965.* Hazard Adams and Leroy Searle, eds. Tallahassee: University Presses of Florida, 1986.

Clark, T.J. *The Painting of Modern Life: Paris in the Art of Manet and his Followers.* Princeton, NJ: Princeton University Press, 1984.

Connor, Steven. *Postmodernist Culture: An Introduction to Theories of the Contemporary.* Oxford: Basil Blackwell, Ltd., 1989.

Crow, Thomas. *Modern Art in the Common Culture.* New Haven and London: Yale University Press, 1996.

Cuddon, J.A. *A Dictionary of Literary Terms.* Rev. ed. New York: Viking Penguin, Inc., 1979.

Davis, Robert Con, ed. *Contemporary Literary Criticism: Modernism through Poststructuralism.* New York: Longmans, Inc., 1986.

De Lauretis, Teresa. "Upping the Anti [sic] in Feminist Theory." In Simon During, ed. *The Cultural Studies Reader.* London and New York: Routledge, 1993.

Eagleton, Terry. *Against the Grain: Essays, 1975-1985.* London: Verso, 1986.

——————— *Literary Theory: An Introduction.* Minneapolis: University of Minnesota Press, 1983.

——————— *The Significance of Theory.* Oxford: Basil Blackwell, Ltd., 1990.

Egbert, Donald Drew. *Social Radicalism and the Arts: Western Europe.* New York: Alfred A. Knopf, 1970.

Fillingham, Lydia Alix. *Foucault for Beginners.* New York: Writers and Readers Publishing, Inc., 1993.

Flew, Anthony, editorial consultant. *A Dictionary of Philosophy.* Rev. 2d ed. New York: St. Martin's Press, 1984.

Foucault, Michel. *The Archaeology of Knowledge & The Discourse on Language.* Trans. A.M. Sheridan Smith. New York: Pantheon Books, 1972.

Fowler, Roger. *A Dictionary of Modern Critical Terms.* Rev. and enl. ed. London and New York: Routledge & Kegan Paul, 1987.

Giddens, Anthony. *Modernity and Self-Identity.* Stanford: Stanford University Press, 1991.

Groden, Michael, and Martin Kreiswirth, eds. *The Johns Hopkins Guide to Literary Theory & Criticism.* Baltimore and London: The Johns Hopkins University Press, 1994.

Habermas, Jürgen. *Philosophical Discourse of Modernity: Twelve Lectures.* Trans. Frederick G. Lawrence. Cambridge, MA: The MIT Press, 1987.

Hammond, Michael, Jane Howarth, and Russell Kent. *Understanding Phenomenology.* Oxford: Basil Blackwell, 1991.

Harris, Wendell V. *Dictionary of Concepts in Literary Criticism and Theory.* New York: Greenwood Press, 1992.

Harvey, David. *The Condition of Postmodernity: An Inquiry into the Origins of Cultural Change.* Oxford: Basil Blackwell, Ltd., 1989.

Hawkes, Terence. *Structuralism & Semiotics.* Berkeley and Los Angeles: University of California Press, 1977.

Holub, Renate. *Antonio Gramsci: Beyond Marxism and Postmodernism.* London: Routledge, 1992.

Homer, William Innes. "Visual Culture: A New Paradigm." *American Art* 12 (Spring, 1998): 6-9.

Horkheimer, Max, and Theodor W. Adorno. *Dialectic of Enlightenment.* Trans. John Cumming. New York: Continuum, 1990.

Jackson, Leonard. *The Poverty of Structuralism: Literature and Structuralist Theory.* New York: Longman Press, 1991.

Jameson, Fredric. *The Political Unconscious: Narrative as a Socially Symbolic Act.* Ithaca, NY: Cornell University Press, 1981.

Jardine, Alice A. *Gynesis: Configurations of Woman and Modernity.* Ithaca, NY: Cornell University Press, 1985.

Jay, Martin. *The Dialectical Imagination: A History of the Frankfurt School and the Institute for Social Research, 1923-1950.* Boston: Little, Brown and Company, 1973.

——————— . *Marxism and Totality: The Adventures of a Concept from Lukács to Habermas.* Berkeley: University of California Press, 1984.

Jencks, Charles. *Postmodernism: The New Classicism in Art and Architecture.* New York: Rizzoli, 1987.

Kristeva, Julia. *Powers of Horror: An Essay on Abjection.* New York: Columbia University Press, 1982.

Kurzweil, Edith. *The Age of Structuralism: Lévi-Strauss to Foucault.* New York: Columbia University Press, 1980.

Lash, Scott. *Sociology of Postmodernism.* London and New York: Routledge, 1990.

Lukács, Georg. *History and Class Consciousness: Studies in Marxist Dialectics.* Trans. Rodney Livingston. Cambridge, MA: The MIT Press, 1971.

Lunn, Eugene. *Marxism and Modernism: An Historical Study of Lukács, Brecht, Benjamin and Adorno.* Berkeley: University of California Press, 1982.

Lyotard, Jean-François. *The Postmodern Condition: A Report on Knowledge.* Trans. Geoff Bennington and Brian Massumi. Minneapolis: University of Minnesota Press, 1984.

Marshall, Gordon. *The Concise Oxford Dictionary of Sociology.* Oxford and New York: Oxford University Press, 1994.

Makaryk, Irena, ed. and comp. *Encyclopedia of Contemporary Literary Theory.* Toronto, Buffalo, and London: University of Toronto Press, 1993.

Mitchell, W.J.T. *Picture Theory: Essays on Verbal and Visual Representation.* Chicago: University of Chicago Press, 1994.

Moriarty, Michael. *Roland Barthes.* Stanford, CA: Stanford University Press, 1991.

Nelson, Cary, and Lawrence Grossberg. *Marxism and the Interpretation of Culture.* Urbana and Chicago: University of Illinois Press, 1988.

Neville, Robert C. *The Highroad around Modernism.* Albany: State University of New York Press, 1992.

Norris, Christopher, and Andrew Benjamin. *What is Deconstruction?* London: Academy Editions, and New York: St. Martin's Press, 1988.

Owens, Craig. *Beyond Recognition: Representation, Power, and Culture.* Berkeley, Los Angeles, Oxford: University of California Press, 1993.

Preminger, Alex, and T.V.F. Brogan. *The New Princeton Encyclopedia of Poetry and Poetics.* Princeton: Princeton University Press, 1993.

Rose, Margaret. *The Post-modern and the Post-industrial.* Cambridge: Cambridge University Press, 1991.

Rosenau, Pauline Marie. *Post-Modernism and the Social Sciences: Insights, Inroads, and Intrusions.* Princeton: Princeton University Press, 1992.

Runes, Dagobert D., ed. *Dictionary of Philosophy.* New York: Philosophical Library, 1983.

Sarup, Madan. *An Introductory Guide to Post-Structuralism and Postmodernism.* Athens, GA: The University of Georgia Press, 1989.

Smart, Barry. *Modern Conditions, Postmodern Controversies.* London and New York: Routledge, 1992.

Sontag, Susan. "Notes on Camp." *Partisan Review* 31 (Fall 1964): 515-30.

Stafford, Barbara Maria. *Good Looking: Essays on the Virtue of Images.* Cambridge, MA: MIT Press, 1996.

Storey, John. *An Introductory Guide to Cultural Theory and Popular Culture.* Athens, GA: University of Georgia Press, 1993.

Tiffin, Chris, and Alan Lawson, eds. *Describing Empire: Post-Colonialism and Textuality.* London: Routledge, 1994.

White, Hayden. "Michel Foucault." In *Structuralism and Since: From Lévi-Strauss to Derrida.* Ed. John Sturrock. Oxford and New York: Oxford University Press, 1979.